Advanced Dungeons&Dragons

™

Official Game Adventure

Dragons of Desolation
by Tracy Hickman and Michael Dobson

TABLE OF CONTENTS

CREDITS

Story: Tracy Hickman
Game Design: Harold Johnson, Bruce Nesmith,
    Michael Dobson, Tracy Hickman
Development/Editing: Michael Dobson and
    Anne Gray
Product Design: Elizabeth Riedel
Cover Art: Keith Parkinson
Interior Art (Pencils): Larry Elmore
Interior Arts (Inks): Jeff Butler
Cartography: Dave "Diesel" LaForce and
    Billy Clemons

Distributed to the book trade in the United States by Random House, Inc., and in Canada by Random House of Canada, Ltd. Distributed to the toy and hobby trade by regional distributors. Distributed in the United Kingdom by TSR(UK)Ltd.
ADVANCED DUNGEONS & DRAGONS, AD&D, DRAGONLANCE, and PRODUCTS OF YOUR IMAGINATION are trademarks of TSR, Inc.

TSR, Inc.
POB 756
Lake Geneva
WI 53147

TSR, Inc.
PRODUCTS OF YOUR IMAGINATION™

TSR(UK)Ltd.
The Mill, Rathmore Road
Cambridge CB14AD
United Kingdom

Printed in U.S.A.
ISBN 0-88038-089-6
9139

since the Cataclysm. Curse the High Priest of Istar for his pride! For in trying to command the Gods rather than begging humbly for their aid, he called down their wrath. The Gods punished Krynn with fire and flood, and much is forever lost. The greatest loss was knowledge of the Gods themselves—the world of Krynn has sunk into blasphemy lo these many generations, and clerics have lost the power to heal.

Mankind's separation from the True Gods opened the door to renewed evil. Dragons, thought to be only a myth to frighten children, are once again in the world. They are commanded by humans called Dragon Highmasters, and assisted by strange creatures called Draconians.

The Dragonarmies have now conquered much of Krynn, and soon all the land will be under their sway. Evil, it seems, may soon triumph over good.

Through my Crystal Globe of Wisdom, I can send my spirit across the land to gather knowledge. And so I have found a glimmer of hope.

Five years ago, seven adventurers set out from the town of Solace to seek the True Gods. They did not succeed. In time, six returned: Tanis, Flint, Tasslehoff, Raistlin, Caramon, and Sturm. Of Kitiara, the seventh, beloved of Tanis, nothing was heard.

On their return, they met Goldmoon, a princess of the Que-Shu tribe, and her lover Riverwind. Goldmoon had a blue crystal staff that could heal by magic.

As the Dragonarmies marched, the Innfellows sought the secret of the staff. Their quest led them to the ancient sunken city of Xak Tsaroth, there to confront an enemy out of nightmare: a Black Dragon.

The crystal staff was indeed a gift of the Gods. With its power, the dragon was destroyed. The Innfellows recovered the Disks of Mishakal, the writings of the Gods, and so did knowledge of the True Gods return to Krynn.

Now armed with powerful weapons of the spirit, the heroes returned to Solace, only to find it overrun by the Dragonarmy. The people had been taken to a terrible slavery in the fortress of Pax Tharkas.

At grave risk and through great heroism, the heroes crept into Pax Tharkas, foiled the plans of the Dragon Highmaster Verminaard, and rescued over 800 slaves.

Through the trackless wilderness, pursued by the tireless draconians, they sought passage through the long-lost dwarven kingdom of Thorbardin to the seaport of Tarsis in the south. Temporary refuge for the escaped slaves was found in the Hopeful Vale, and the heroes braved the dangers of Skullcap, the fortress of the evil wizard Fistandantilus, who perished in the Dwarfgate War.

On that trek, the Seeker priest Elistan became the second true cleric of Krynn. And so did the High God Paladine reenter the world of Krynn.

And there, deep beneath Skullcap, was found the key that would unlock the gates to Thorbardin...

FROM THE ICONOCHRONOS OF ASTINUS OF PALANTHUS, LOREKEEPER OF KRYNN, IN THE 351ST YEAR AFTER THE CATACLYSM.

notes for the dungeonmaster

"Dragons of Desolation" is the fourth in the epic DRAGONLANCE™ series, and concludes the First Book of Dragonlance: Tales of Autumn Twilight.

DRAGONLANCE is a story. The modules in this series should ideally be played as a continuing saga. Players are encouraged to take on the roles of the main heroes in this epic; the Character Cards can be cut out and used by the players.

You may allow players to bring other characters into this adventure. If so, adjust those characters so they conform to the world of Krynn, which is unlike most AD&D™ worlds. (See THE WORLD OF KRYNN, below.)

If you allow players to bring in other characters, but still want to play the epic, the DRAGONLANCE characters must be either player characters (PCs) or non-player characters (NPCs). If players wish to play multiple characters, make sure that they play each character as an individual. Some characters can be used as Henchmen NPCs—for example, one player should play both Goldmoon and Riverwind, one (their choice) as a Henchman NPC.

If players do not choose to take all of the DRAGONLANCE heroes, you should keep the others in the background as NPCs. All of the pre-generated characters figure prominently in future modules.

In any case, it's a good idea to keep the party to a manageable size.

Three NPCs require particular attention. Laurana, Princess of Qualinost, was rescued from Pax Tharkas in DL 2. In DL 6 she becomes a PC. Although she should be in the background in DL 4, make sure the other PCs (especially Tanis and Gilthanas) are aware of her presence.

Elistan was converted from the false Seeker religion to the worship of the true gods, and is now a powerful cleric. In DL 6, he becomes a PC. In this module, he enters the dream world to battle Verminaard, and does not reappear until the climax.

Eben Shatterstone, the third important NPC, is a traitor, an agent of Verminaard. Eben is self-serving and greedy rather than actively evil, and so his alignment is neutral. Eben was introduced to the party in DL 2 as the victim of a draconian attack. The attack was a fake. Until he betrays the heroes in the final chapter of this adventure, he appears to support the party in every way. Give his Character Card to one of the players to run as an NPC. Overrule any obviously out-of-character behavior. When Eben's treason occurs, take the card back and run him for the remainder of the adventure.

If you don't want to play the DRAGONLANCE epic, you can adapt this adventure to your own campaign.

DRAGONLANCE is a complex saga. To run it well, you must read this module carefully to visualize the story, and to think of what players may do. You must motivate the players subtly so that they follow the right path. Sometimes, you must improvise to keep the story on track.

Because DRAGONLANCE is a story, both heroes and villains often figure prominently in later modules. If "name" charac-ters or villains should be killed, arrange "obscure deaths" for them. Their bodies should not be found. Think up a creative explanation for their "miraculous" survival. For example, a character tumbles down a 500 foot shaft to certain death. Several modules later, the character reappears with a story about how he landed on a ledge and was knocked out. Much later, he came to, and spent weeks recovering and escaping. Some characters can die permanently. When a "name" character no longer plays a part in the story, his death can occur. Player characters brought into this adventure from outside can be killed normally.

The player characters are variously referred to as PCs, adventurers, heroes, and companions. Boxed sections of text are read aloud when the PCs experience that Encounter or Event.

If you are playing DL 4 without having played the previous DL modules, you must set the stage for the current adventure by using the chapter of the *Iconochronos* on the opposite page. If you have played the DL modules up to this point, no additional background is needed—the story starts the morning after the end of DL 3.

Sometimes, a character must make an Ability Check against one of his Character Abilities (Strength, Dexterity, Wisdom, etc.). The player rolls 1d20. If the result is equal to or less than the player's Ability score in the appropriate area, the Check succeeds. For example, a PC with a Dexterity of 15 makes a Dexterity Check by rolling 1d20. If the result is 15 or less, the Check succeeds; if the result is 16 or more, the Check fails.

the world of krynn

There are important differences between the world of Krynn and standard AD&D campaigns. Characters who have adventured in previous DL modules know the following information. Players and characters new to the world should be given this background.

True clerics have been unknown in Krynn for centuries. Most clerics do not have spell powers, since they worship false gods. True clerics wear a Medallion of Faith bearing the symbol of a god or goddess. When a new true cleric comes into being, the medallion magically duplicates, and the new medallion bears the symbol of the appropriate god or goddess. Only two of the true gods are currently known: Mishakal, goddess of healing, and Paladine, the high god of good. All PC clerics brought into the campaign must be of good

alignment and worship one of these two gods.

All PC elves in this adventure are from Qualinesti elves. Other elves — the Sylvanesti — appear in later modules.

The equivalent of a halfling in Krynn is a Kender. Kender look like wizened 14-year-olds and (unlike halflings) wear shoes. See Tasslehoff Burrfoot's Character Card for more information.

The values of gold and other trade items are completely different in this world. Gold is much less valuable; steel is the main trade metal. One steel piece (stl) is equivalent to 1 standard gp in purchasing power. PCs that enter Krynn from other campaigns do not automatically trade their gold pieces for steel pieces—they may find their personal wealth greatly altered!

The following exchange rates apply in all lands encountered in this module:
1 gpw (gold piece weight) of steel=10 gp, or 20 sp, or 100 cp, or 2 ip (iron pieces), or 1/5 pp, or 2 bp (bronze pieces).

Finally, dragons have been absent from Krynn for nearly 1,000 years. They are considered merely legends by all who have not personally beheld them. Characters may be thought foolish, or liars, if they talk about dragons to the wrong people.

Chapter 14: The Doors of Thorbardin

Events

Each Chapter is divided into Encounters (keyed to areas) and Events (keyed to time). Keep track of both location and time to know which Event or Encounter to run next.

The Mission

Eight hundred refugees are fleeing the armies of the dragon highmaster. They were forced to enter a wilderness ringed by impassable mountains. The only route to safety is through the ancient dwarven kingdom of Thorbardin—but the gates to Thorbardin have been hidden for over 300 years. The PCs must find the gates to Thorbardin, get permission for the refugees to cross through, and get back before the dragonarmies attack the refugee camp.

About Time

The dragonarmies conquer areas of the wilderness on a regular basis. If you played DL 2 and DL 3, use those modules to calculate the time available to the refugees. If not, assume that the heroes have seven days to complete their quest. Do not tell the players how much time they have. The Epilogue tells what happens if the heroes succeed...or fail!

Event #1: Departure of Elistan

The adventure begins in the camp of the refugees at midnight—the same night as the end of DL 3.

> You are summoned to a late night meeting of the refugees Council of Freedom. When you arrive, you notice that Elistan seems strangely peaceful. "The dragonarmies are approaching, and now you must find the way to the gates of Thorbardin. It is the only hope for our people. There is little time; waste none of it. As for me, I now know what must be done," he says.
>
> "To the hope of safety!" he says, lifts a flagon, and drinks.

Although the flagon contains only water, as soon as Elistan drinks, he grows pale and shudders once. Then, eyes rolling back, he pitches forward.

Elistan has received a dream vision from Paladine, and has gone into the dream world to battle Verminaard. The PCs do not learn this until the end of the module.

Elistan cannot be revived by any means available to the party. He appears dead, but his body does not decay.

The Council asks the PCs to leave in the morning to find a way through Thorbardin. If the characters found a map to the gates in DL 3, they know where to go—otherwise, Fizban the Fabulous (see **NPC Capsules**) now reveals that he knows exactly where the gates are.

Event #2: Dreams of Darkness

This Event takes place the same night as Event #1, as soon as the heroes fall asleep. All sleeping characters have the following dream:

> You are standing in front of a huge door. You feel that there is great evil behind it. The voice of Elistan, now very weak, is calling for you.
>
> "I have entered this door and cannot find my way back," he cries. "Please! Come and bring that which I left behind!" He does not seem able to hear anything you say; he just repeats his cry over and over again.

Ask each player in turn if he will open the door. If all characters refuse, the dream ends and the PCs awake. Skip Event #3, below. If even one character opens the door, read the next boxed section.

You feel yourself floating in a vast nothingness for an uncertain length of time—whether moments or centuries, you cannot tell. Suddenly, you are standing on an empty plain. In the distance, mountains are silhouetted against a starry sky. Before you is a tower made of crystal, silver, and pure white marble. Beside you are your companions in adventure.

You walk toward the tower. The ground is soft beneath your feet and a sweet, warm wind blows. But as you walk, the tower changes. Now it is made of steel and stone, and the wind is bitter. And now it is made of rough, decaying stone, and the tower is in ruins.

There are seven open archways into the tower. As you watch, a group of hooded pilgrims approaches. As they come closer, they begin to change into draconians, but do not attack. They enter the tower.

You see a long, dimly glowing tunnel that leads inside. You and your companions enter...and suddenly find yourself in a large chamber!

Seven hallways radiate from this room. Six are brightly lit; one is dim. From the dim hall whispers the voice of Elistan: "I have entered this door and cannot come back. Please! Follow me and bring that which I left behind!"

In the six bright hallways are your heart's desires—glory, power, wealth. But you know that your doom lies down the dim corridor.

Suddenly, you wake in a cold sweat, deeply disturbed. Something horrible happened to you and your companions ...but you can't remember what!

Event #3: The Dragon Highlord Arrives

This Event takes place the following morning. If no hero opened the door, the Event does not occur.

Out of the setting sun comes a dark shadow and a rush of wind. It is a huge red dragon, its wings terribly scarred. Astride it is the dragon highlord of Pax Tharkas—Verminaard!

The huge dragon hovers above you, its mammoth wings beating slowly.

Verminaard (see **NPC Capsules**) calls for the heroes, using both voice and telepathy. "Pitiful fools," he sneers, "to think you could defeat me in the Mind of Evil!"

When Verminaard uses the phrase, "The Mind of Evil," each of the heroes suddenly remembers the terrible dream of the night before.

Memories flood into your mind. In the dream, you walk down the dim corridor, afraid and despairing. Each step you take is harder than the last. At last you enter a large chamber.

There, before you, stands Verminaard, holding Elistan prisoner in a crystal cage. A small golden lock holds the cage shut. Elistan sees you, and tries to speak, but cannot.

Verminaard raises his hand. Out of the darkness step fearsome fighters. He laughs, and lowers his hand in a chopping motion. The fighters attack!

Give each player one of the Dream Cards on pp. 6 and 7. Once the players have read their dream cards, Verminaard laughs chillingly. "So, fools, now you remember your night in the Mind of Evil!"

The dragon highlord speaks to each member of the party, revealing that he knows exactly what happened to each person in the dream. He mocks the futile efforts of the heroes to resist him, and belittles their accomplishments both in the dream and in the real world. He gloats of his victories and their defeats.

"It is pointless for you to continue in this lost cause," he says. "Wealth and power can be yours if you but take your place beside me, and place your swords in my service."

Verminaard has no intention of keeping his word. If the heroes betray the refugees, Verminaard takes them back to Pax Tharkas with promises of rich rewards. Once there, he orders his troops to feed them to Ember.

If the heroes attack, Ember flies out of missile range. Verminaard laughs at the futility of the attack. If the heroes actually hit either Verminaard or the dragon, Ember attacks with spells, but does not use his breath weapon.

If the heroes reject Verminaard's offer, he says, "Fools! I could destroy you as you stand. But I have other uses for you...and there are things worse than death!"

With that, he commands the dragon to fly off to the north.

Event #4: The Dwarven Gates

After Event #3 (or the next morning, if Event #3 does not occur), the Council urges the PCs to seek out the dwarven gates without delay. Using the map from DL 3 (or the instructions given by Fizban, who goes with the party in any case), the PCs reach the doors after four hours' travel. Run normal wilderness random encounters. After four hours' travel, the heroes see the following...

The steep defile suddenly opens up onto a narrow, 5 foot wide ledge. Below, a cliff drops 1,000 feet to the valley. Above, the

cliff climbs 500 feet to become part of the mountain range. Another defile can be seen at the far end of the ledge, almost 100 feet away.

A large secret door is in the middle of this cliff face, so well hidden that there is only a 15% chance that it can be found by non-elven races. Elves and half-elves have normal chances to find the door. If the PCs have a map, they know that the door is supposed to be here.

The defile on the far side of the ledge leads into a box canyon dead end.

If the PCs cannot find the door, Fizban locates it for them.

The following methods can open the great door:

1. A *fireball* spell can open the door. If Fizban is with the party, he tells everyone to stand back, then casts his *fireball*. Fizban stupidly stands right in front of the door, and appears to be destroyed in the blast. The door slowly opens (see below).

2. A *knock* spell can open the door. Fizban does not use that spell.

3. The door-opening mechanism is found. If any elf or half-elf character successfully checks for secret doors a second time, he finds a small (2 feet square) door that is easily opened. Within the door is a small opening with a mechanical hand in it. If any character shakes the hand, the door slowly opens.

When the door begins to open, a deep rumbling sound (like an earthquake) is heard. The ledge and cliff face begins to shake. The door suddenly breaks free and pushes out 5 feet; anyone standing in front of it must make a Dexterity Check to avoid falling off the cliff. No matter how the door is opened, Fizban manages to be caught on the ledge, and falls down, apparently to his death. His body cannot be found. The door continues to move outward at a rate of 5 feet per round.

The door is built on a giant screw shaft propelled by a mechanism within the mountain. Originally, the door would rest on the wide ledge that once was here. However, during the Cataclysm, much of the ledge collapsed. Therefore, after the door has moved out 15 feet, the machinery begins to strain. Strange noises are heard. Within 3 segments, the screw shaft breaks, and the door, which weighs several tons, plunges over the cliff face, falling 1,000 feet and crushing anything beneath it.

The entrance to the lost dwarven kingdom of Thorbardin has been found. The door, once opened, remains open forever.

Dream Card — Tanis

Fierce draconian warriors attack, and you are consumed with battlelust! You draw your sword, and strike about you, cutting down your enemies.

Great elation fills your heart as you see Kitiara, the great love of your life, fighting at your side! You know that you are unbeatable, and that victory is in your grasp.

You realize suddenly that if you strike the golden lock with your sword, Elistan will be freed and Verminaard forever destroyed. But you must act now, for Verminaard is moving to take Elistan with him into the darkness!

As you lunge forward, you hear Kitiara cry for help. You turn, and see her sorely beset by draconians. Without your help, it is obvious she will lose. You hesitate, torn between your duty and your love.

At that moment, a draconian drives a spear deep into your chest. You fall; your last blood-dimmed sight is of Kitiara dying at the hands of the draconians.

© 1984 TSR, Inc.

Dream Card — Goldmoon

Out of the darkness come fierce warriors—members of your own Que-Shu tribe, murdered by draconians! You see their expressionless faces, and realize that they are lost to evil.

You fight because you must, but tears run down your cheeks as you cut down people you loved dearly. Despair, guilt, and horror oppress your soul. Yet you fight on. Around you your comrades die, one by one. You feel that the True Gods have abandoned you.

Suddenly you know what you must do. You step forward, and with a mighty blow shatter the glass case. Elistan steps out, looks at you...and then at Verminaard. His eyes become cold, expressionless. You scream, and reach your hand out to him, ignoring the blows that fall upon you. Elistan reaches down to you, grabs the amulet around your neck, and tears it from you.

You collapse, weak and bleeding from the sword-thrusts in your body. As you die, you see Elistan's white robes turn to scarlet as he disappears into the void with Verminaard.

© 1984 TSR, Inc.

Dream Card — Riverwind

Out of the darkness come fierce warriors—members of your own Que-Shu tribe, murdered by draconians! You see their expressionless faces, and realize that they are lost to evil.

You fight because you must, but tears run down your cheeks as you cut down people you loved dearly. Despair, guilt, and horror oppress your soul. Yet you fight on. Around you, your comrades die, one by one.

You see Goldmoon before you, fighting to reach Elistan as your own tribesmen stab her. You are bleeding from your many wounds, yet you shrug off the pain and fight your way toward Goldmoon.

Your legs and arms grow strangely heavy, and you can't seem to get closer to Goldmoon no matter what you do. Despair and anguish stab into your heart as you see her fall, mortally wounded by her own tribesmen.

© 1984 TSR, Inc.

Dream Card — Sturm

Fierce draconian warriors attack, and you are consumed with battlelust! You draw your sword, and strike about you, cutting down your enemies.

Great elation fills your heart as you cut down the draconians surrounding you. You look around to see where you are needed. Magically, a wall rises before you, and you hear guards crying that the draconians are preparing to breach the wall. A huge blue dragon appears in mid-air, demoralizing all who face it. You know that you are the only one who can defeat the dragon. You start toward the wall as trumpets sound the retreat.

But you cannot go forward. Fear such as you have never known stabs into your heart. You know that if you confront this monster you will die.

You turn away, shaking and ashamed. Behind you, the wall is breached and the draconian hordes pour through. The dragon lands.

You do not resist as you are trampled by hordes of draconians pouring through the battlements. Bitterly despairing, you die a coward.

© 1984 TSR, Inc.

Dream Card — Laurana

Fierce draconian warriors attack, and you are consumed with battlelust! You draw your sword, and strike about you, cutting down your enemies.

But the draconian hordes are endless, and around you there is death. Sturm falls beside you, draconians hacking at his body. You look around and see the horror. You falter.

Voices shout at you, asking you what to do. Another voice cries for you to take command. Everyone's eyes are on you; everyone is yelling your name, calling for help.

But you don't want to help. You want to be told what to do. You want to be helped. Finally, you can't stand it any more. You throw down your weapons and run out of the room into the darkness. You run farther, only to find that the darkness grows ...and you cannot stop running.

© 1984 TSR, Inc.

Dream Card — Tika, Gilthanas, and other Fighters

Fierce draconian warriors attack, and you are consumed with battlelust! You draw your sword, and strike about you, cutting down your enemies.

You are determined to prove yourself in this battle, yet things start to go wrong. You stumble, and accidently trip Sturm, who falls under the flashing blades of the draconians. You jostle Raistlin just as he is about to unleash a spell. Your friends are yelling at you to get out of the way, to leave them alone.

Panicked, you look around. Enemies you thought you killed are standing up and attacking. Soon you are fighting through tears of frustration.

You fight on, stubbornly, but your mistakes get worse and worse. Suddenly, you see a huge, armored back—a draconian! You stab deeply, and your aim is true. You wipe tears from your eyes, and, too late, realize that you have stabbed Caramon!

You drop your sword and do not resist as the draconians stab you. You die, falling across Caramon's body.

© 1984 TSR, Inc.

6

Dream Card — Tasslehoff and Other Thieves

Suddenly, battle rages all about you as draconian hordes attack! Your companions can take care of these monsters—only you can free Elistan! Carefully, you make your way to the crystal cage, and inspect the small golden lock. What luck! The lock is childishly simple.

You pull out a lockpick, and go to work. But the lock doesn't yield. You try again, but find that this simple lock resists your best techniques. You hear the sounds of combat behind you, and see your friends begin to die under the onslaught of the draconians.

You know that you can stop the slaughter if you can just open this simple, simple lock! Your hands begin to bleed from tearing at the lock in bitter frustration.

Finally, ignoring your better judgement, you try to force the lock open, but trigger a very simple trap you knew was there all along. As the small, poisoned needle enters your hand, you realize that all is doomed. As the poison courses through your body, you know that this is the end.

© 1984 TSR, Inc.

Dream Card — Caramon

Fierce draconian warriors attack, and you are consumed with battlelust! You draw your sword, and strike about you, cutting down your enemies.

You stand together with your brother Raistlin. His magic protects you as you slay enemies all around you.

You are fearless in your attack, but see your friends, one by one, overwhelmed by the draconian hordes. Yet you stand, and you and Raistlin are able to move toward the caged Elistan.

But suddenly the magic spell protecting you dissipates! You turn to see Raistlin, now dressed in black robes, leaving you for Verminaard. Your beloved brother has abandoned you, and you are bereft. You call his name, but a fierce pain in your back reminds you of the battle.

You have been stabbed in the back, and you cannot see your killer. You pitch forward, dying, your last thoughts with your brother, forever lost to evil.

© 1984 TSR, Inc.

Dream Card — Raistlin and Other Magic-Users

A horde of draconians attack, but you know that your spells will protect you. The magic has never been more strong within you, and you know that today you are capable of feats far beyond what you thought possible. Victory is at hand!

Suddenly, you have a vision of yourself dressed in black robes, feared and respected, rich and powerful. Before you, opened, is the *Book of the Magius*, in which all knowledge of mages throughout time is contained. All you have to do is walk through a door in front of you. You look at your companions, and then at the book. How pitiful they look; how doomed!

Without another glance, you stride through the door, noticing as you do so that your red robes turn black.

© 1984 TSR, Inc.

Dream Card — Flint

Verminaard signals, and a horde of mountain dwarves—your sworn enemies—rushes to the attack. The battlelust sings in your heart as you realize that your revenge is at hand!

But there seems to be an infinite supply of the foul creatures, and you and your fellows are slowly overwhelmed. "I led them into this fate," you think. "I am the oldest, and responsible." Despair and guilt enter your heart as you see your dearest friends perish by the hands of your enemies. There Tasslehoff dies, trying to rescue Elistan, there Tanis dies, and there Caramon dies.

All is hopeless. You keep fighting, now much weaker, as the mountain dwarves continue their assault. You hardly feel the swords cutting into your body. The loss of blood makes you weaker, and finally you fall. Your last thought is of your friends.

© 1984 TSR, Inc.

Dream Card — Clerics Except Goldmoon

A horde of draconians attacks at Verminaard's sign. You call on the True Gods for support, then lay about you, hoping to destroy as many of the vermin as possible.

The draconians continue to come, no matter how many are killed. Despair enters your heart as you realize that you and your companions cannot survive.

Suddenly you know what you must do. You step forward, and with a mighty blow shatter the glass case. Elistan steps out, looks at you...then at Verminaard. His eyes become cold, expressionless. You scream, and reach your hand out to him, ignoring the blows that fall upon you. Elistan reaches down to you, grabs the amulet around your neck, and tears it from you.

You collapse, weak and bleeding from the sword-thrusts in your body. As you die, you see Elistan's white robes turn to scarlet as he disappears into the void with Verminaard.

© 1984 TSR, Inc.

Chapter 15: The North Gate of the Dwarves.

Using the Dwarven Kingdom Maps

The great kingdom of Thorbardin is detailed on the large map. The "Kingdom of Thorbardin" map shows locations of cities, major corridors, lakes, caverns, and the like. Also on the map are the sixteen City Blocks that make up the dwarven cities. All the City Blocks on the map are facing north.

It has been said that if you've seen one dwarven city, you've seen them all. Nothing could be more true. Once a dwarf finds something he likes, he sticks with it. Dwarves leave architectural innovation to the elves, who enjoy that sort of thing. In the world of Krynn, all dwarven cities are made of the same City Blocks, repeated endlessly.

To find your way around a dwarven city, a third type of map is used. This map resembles a crossword puzzle, made up of small boxes with numbers and letters in them.

Each chapter has one or more "crossword puzzle" maps in it. Each box on the map represents one of the sixteen City Blocks on the large map.

In each box is a place for a Block Number (one of the sixteen city block types), Facing (a compass direction: N, E, S, or W, or "R" for Random), and Encounter (keyed to the Encounter section of the chapter). All boxes have a City Block Number and a Facing; only some of them have Encounters.

The left box in the example on pg. 10 contains a "2" and an "E." On the large map,

"2" is a Great Hall. (Remember, all City Blocks on the large map are facing north.) Since the direction is "E," rotate the block 90 degrees so that the City Block faces east. It connects with a "8 E." Looking again at the large map, you see that "8" is a Court. Since it, too, faces north on the large map, you must rotate it to face east. The court contains an Encounter, as well. Refer to the current chapter's Encounter section to find out what happens in the Court.

(NOTE: If the direction is "R," assign a facing at random.)

Some areas of the dwarven kingdom are currently inhabited, others are in ruins. Modify the block descriptions below based on the information in each chapter.

City Blocks are connected to each other by the little extensions on each block, which are open. If the City Block doesn't connect with anything, the extensions are just alcoves.

Some of the cities of Thorbardin are not visited in this adventure. You can create your own dwarven cities just by preparing "crossword puzzle" maps, and set your own adventures therein.

City Block Descriptions

The sixteen dwarven City Blocks are described below. Some areas of the kingdom are currently inhabited and active. In those areas, use the full description. Some areas are deserted and lie in ruins. In those areas, machinery

does not work and everything is covered with the dust of centuries. In the Northgate area, scars of the Dwarfgate War are everywhere: skeletons, rusty armor, etc. Nothing is of use to the players.

Because it is important for the heroes to get through the dwarven kingdom quickly, not a lot of detail is provided for the various cities. Keep the characters on track as they move through the kingdom. If they wander into areas not described, or need a level of detail not provided in the explanations, you must improvise to fit the situation.

If you decide to create additional adventures in the halls of the dwarves, you can add whatever additional detail you need to the City Blocks.

City Block 1. Gatehouse

Gatehouse blocks control access to the dwarven city. The immense gate is powered by a water-driven machine that turns a huge screw.

City Block 2. Great Hall

The Great Hall forms the main street of a dwarven kingdom. Merchant shops line the passage.

City Block 3. Kings Wall Corner I

The Kings Wall is an inner defense for the dwarven city. It is made up of City Blocks 3-7.

The Kings Wall is generally an upper-class area, filled with expensive inns, homes of the rich, and lush temples.

If there is a city level below a Kings Wall block, then the pit drops through to the next level, 100 feet below. If there is no level underneath, the pit is 50 feet deep.

The temple in this block is used by visitors to the city, rather than by city residents.

City Block 4. kings Wall Gate

The Kings Wall Gate controls access to the inner city. The drawbridge is made of wood and can be burned (10 rounds until collapse) or removed by soldiers (this takes 5 rounds).

Beyond the drawbridge are heavy iron doors and portcullises lined with arrow slits on either side.

In inhabited areas, guards are stationed at the drawbridge and also occupy the guard houses inside the wall.

City Block 5. kings Wall I

In this block are the homes and temples of the upper class. If this block is above another city block, the air moat opens onto the level below — otherwise it drops into water 20 feet below the floor.

City Block 6. kings Wall II

This block contains upper-class homes, temples, and shops.

City Block 7. kings Wall Corner II

This area is similar to City Block 3, above.

City Block 8. Court of Thanes

The royal court is lined with sculpture and tapestry — the finest art of the dwarven kingdom.

The seven thrones are for the Seven Ruling Thanes Under the Mountain, the rulers of each of the major dwarf races. Once there was a High King of Thorbardin, but since the days of Derkin, no one has risen to claim the throne.

This block also contains quarters for visiting thanes, and temples for use by the court. Government offices are also located here.

City Block 9. Residence

Most dwarves live in residence blocks. A few stores operate in the residence blocks, but goods are mostly purchased elsewhere.

City Block 10. Transport Shaft

The Transport Shafts are the primary method of travel between levels in the dwarven kingdom. The central circular chamber is a shaft that stretches through many levels above and below.

Driven by a mechanism at the bottom of the shaft (City Block 15), chain ladders and great hanging buckets move up on one side and down on the other. Platforms lead out over the pit so that it is easy for a traveler to step into one of the buckets as it moves slowly by, and then to step off when the desired level is reached.

In deserted areas of the dwarven kingdom, the shafts are abandoned and the driving mechanisms disengaged. The chains and buckets do not move unless someone climbs on, and then only allow downward movement. The chains cannot be climbed unless the locking mechanism in City Block 15 is engaged.

To get onto the chain or into a bucket in a deserted area, a character must jump 10 feet from the edge and catch a chain. This requires a Dexterity Check. If the Check succeeds, he descends slowly. If the Check fails, the player makes a second Check to arrest the fall. If that Check succeeds, he catches a chain, but takes 2d6 points of damage. If the second Check fails, a third Check is made. If the third Check succeeds, the character falls 30 feet before catching a chain and takes 3d6 of damage, but then descends normally. If the third Check fails, the character falls the full distance of the shaft and takes normal falling damage of 1d6 (cumulative) per 10 feet fallen to a maximum of 20d6.

The Transport Block is the center of dwarven life. Assembly halls are the homes of plays and music. Major bazaars and shops are located here. There are also smaller public worship halls and guildhalls for the dwarven artisans.

City Block 11. Wharf

Dwarven cities sometimes open onto underground lakes and rivers. The dwarves have sometimes carried on trade by water, and occasionally fish.

The wharf area contains boat slips, warehouses, government offices, and repair facilities for boats.

City Block 12. Great Temple

The dwarves of Thorbardin are among the few races of post-Cataclysm Krynn to retain knowledge of the true gods. The primary god of the mountain dwarves is Reorx, the forger.

According to dwarven religion, the holy kingdom of Reorx is located far beneath the earth. If the temple is located above another City Block, the pit opens up onto the next level—otherwise it is at least 1,000 feet deep, for the dwarves believe the deeper the shaft, the more holy the temple.

Climbing down a Shaft of Reorx would be considered a sacrilege to a dwarf.

In a typical Temple Block there are small stores selling religious items. Dwarven clerics normally live in a Temple Block, and have a private temple in the block for their own use.

City Block 13. Dungeons

Although fierce in battle, the dwarves take pride in the taking of prisoners.

The dungeons have cell areas accessed through special rooms called Transit Areas. A special mechanism controlled from the guard area operates first one portcullis, then the other, serving as an "airlock" to control access to the cell blocks. A key is required to operate the mechanism. Outside the cell area are guard quarters and weapons storage areas.

The internal areas are the cells proper, including dining and exercise facilities. Not all cells were locked, depending on the status and behavior of the prisoner, since exit from the cell area is so tightly controlled. If Cell Blocks are adjacent, there is frequently free movement between them, but all connection with the outside is still controlled by the guards.

City Block 14. Smithy

In the great smithies, the dwarves of ages past created wondrous works. Stone troughs convey metal from the central furnace to the many stalls where dwarven craftsmen work. A large cauldron hangs over the central firepit, controlled by complex machinery. The cauldron can be swiveled, tipped, or pulled out of the fire to be filled. The floor of the firepit is covered in several feet of soot and ashes. The floors and walls of the smithy are streaked with hardened bits of metal and scorch marks.

City Block 15. Transport Machinery

The large pit in the central chamber is filled with the machinery that operates the transport system. A net is suspended above the machinery. The net serves two purposes: it can reduce falling damage by 50%, and protects the machinery from anything falling into it.

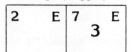

2	E	7 3	E

Northgate

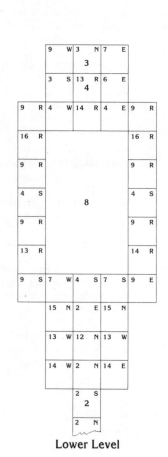

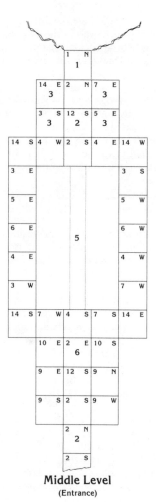

n

Lower Level

Middle Level
(Entrance)

(Upper Level)

City Block 16. Gardens

These beautiful, well-kept gardens are the parks of the dwarven realms. They are lighted by shafts of crystal leading to the surface (a primitive fiber optics system). The garden contains small trees, shrubs, mushrooms, and fungi.

Encounters in the Northgate

There are both random and set encounters in Northgate. Use the Random Encounter Chart on the inside cover to determine random encounters for each City Block in Northgate. Whenever the Chart indicates that a random encounter will take place, roll 1d8. Each City Block has the numbers 1-8 on it. The encounter is located at the number of the die result, *e.g.*, a roll of "6" means that the encounter takes place in Location 6 in the appropriate City Block.)

The heroes may decide to bring the refugees along with them into Thorbardin. If they do, 20 derro of the Theiwar Kingdom (also known as Dark Dwarves) attack 1d6 turns after the refugees enter Northgate. An additional 20 Theiwar attack each 1d6 turns. After three attacks, if the heroes have not already decided to have the refugees retreat, the refugee council decides to turn back. The refugees make camp outside of Northgate to wait for the heroes' return with permission to enter. The refugees have heard many awful rumors about the dwarves of Thorbardin, and are very fearful.

Because the refugees have now moved further from the approaching dragonarmies, the heroes have an additional 48 hours to get passage through Thorbardin.

All drawbridges in Northgate are down and can be crossed. The drawbridge mechanism is rusted and cannot be repaired.

1. Dwarfgate

> The scars of fierce battle streak the walls. The floor is littered with broken shards of pottery and rusted metal. Ancient wagons, their axles broken, litter the major corridors. The skeletons of dwarves and men lie where they died so long ago, clothed in rusted armor and rags, silent witnesses to the terrible conflict that once raged in these halls.

Everything is deserted and in ruins. There are no random encounters in this block. The mechanism that once operated the doors is rusted and broken.

2. Arman Kharas

If this encounter has already occured, do not repeat it.

> An armed party of dwarves steps into the corridor before you. The leader, strength and confidence lining his features, steps forward. The large hammer at his side is held loose but ready. He rumbles, "What business have you strangers among the halls of the Hylar?"

The leader is named Arman Kharas (see **NPC Capsules**). There are 12 Hylar dwarves, each wearing chain mail and carrying shield and war hammer, in his party.

If the heroes attack, the party fights fiercely and if it looks like the Hylar will be beaten, Arman will surrender. If the heroes talk, Arman listens to their story, though his men remain ready to fight.

If the heroes treat Arman with respect and honor, he decides to take them before the Court of the Thanes for judgment. There, they might be granted safe passage. If the heroes are disrespectful, Arman orders them out of Thorbardin and attacks if they refuse.

Normally, the Hylar avoid Northgate, since it is held by the Theiwar dwarves, sworn enemies of the Hylar. However, the Theiwar have captured Arman's half-brother Pick, and Arman is searching the halls of Northgate for him. If the heroes offer to help Arman rescue his half-brother, Arman takes them to the Court of the Thanes even if they are disrespectful.

Arman has an idea where Pick may be held (see Encounter 4), and leads the heroes toward the dungeon if they agree to help him.

Once Pick has been rescued, Arman leads the heroes to the City of the Hylar (Chapter 16) by the most direct route.

It is very important that the heroes accompany Arman and do not fight him. Encourage peaceful negotiation and highlight Arman's good intentions and behavior.

3. The Dark Guide

If this encounter has already occured, do not repeat it.

> A stunted dwarf, pale of skin and with large eyes, sits mumbling to himself and pulling at his hair. He is clothed in black oily rags with bits of leather and metal sewn into them. He looks up, then begins to cower before you.

This is Krothgar, a Theiwar, recently ousted by his clan for cowardice.

If he is offered food or safety, he agrees to guide the party through the dwarven kingdom. Actually, he plans to guide the party to the Theiwar community on the upper level (Encounter 7), hoping to redeem himself by offering his clan these strangers from the outside world.

4. Prisoners

No random encounters occur in this block. In area 1, two Hylar dwarves are held prisoner—one is Pick, Arman Kharas' half-brother. In area 5 are 2-8 Theiwar guards. In area 8 are other prisoners, including Aghar, Hylar, and Klar dwarves.

If Pick sees the party, he calls out for rescue, and says his family will reward his safe return. The other Hylar dwarf in the cell is dying of a rotting disease, and dies an hour after rescue if nothing is done to cure him.

Once rescued, Pick would gladly lead the party through Thorbardin, but unfortunately doesn't know where he is or how to get home.

5. Anvil's Echo

> A vast cavern opens up before you, spanned by a bridge that leads off into the darkness. The slightest whisper seems to echo endlessly in the black depths. Low stone rails, three feet high, line each side of the wide bridge. The rails are held up by carvings of small dwarves.

The cavern is called the Anvil's Echo. Legend has it that the sound of a dwarven hammer on an anvil will echo for eternity in this dwarf-made cavern. The ceiling is one hundred feet above; the floor of the cavern (Encounter 8) is one hundred feet below.

The bridge is part of the Northgate defense system. Murder holes in the ceiling were used to drop missiles, boiling oil, molten lead, and boulders on attackers—but the defenders of Northgate are long dead.

Halfway across the bridge are two ropers, flattened against the stone guard rails, waiting to ambush the party.

6. Attack of the Theiwar

A clan of Theiwar dwarves are foraging in this block. Unless the party is totally silent, the Theiwar are not surprised. There are 75 Theiwar. As the heroes approach the center of the block, the dark dwarves fill the main hallways to the south and the east.

If the party is being led by Arman Kharas, he races down the west end of the hall shouting for all to follow him. He leads all who follow to the nearest Transport Block, and jumps to catch one of the chains. All of Arman's men follow him onto the chains; they all succeed in catching the chains. See City Block 15 for operation of the transport system.

The Theiwar can ride the chains, but only do so in emergencies. Since they do not see this as an emergency, they do not pursue.

If Krothgar is guiding the party, he runs back in the direction from which he came, since these Theiwar are from a different clan, and would gladly kill him too. Krothgar finds the nearest stair and runs to the upper level, occupied by his own clan. The Theiwar do not pursue into what they consider enemy territory.

7. City of the Theiwar

Krothgar's clan occupies the small walled fort on the upper level of Northgate. There are 250 derro led by a derro savant. If by some stroke of bad luck the party enters the clan fort, the Theiwar try to capture the party, take their possessions, then throw them into the well of the great bridge to their death.

8. Floor of the Anvil's Echo

> A huge, square cavern is carved out of the solid stone. The floor is lined with rubble. Scattered about are skeletons long dead, fallen from the great bridge above.

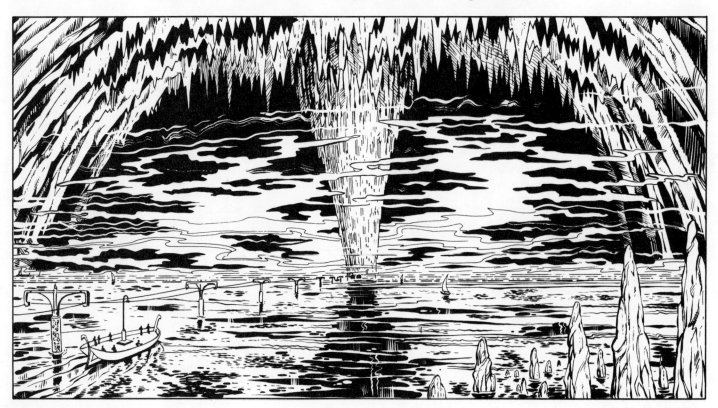

encounters

9. leaving Northgate

If the party leaves Northgate in the company of Arman Kharas, Arman guides them through the dwarven realms to the city of the Hylar by the safest and most direct route. He knows where the Theiwar strongholds are, and avoids them whenever possible. Arman wishes to avoid combat, intending only to get his half-brother Pick to safety and to take the party before the Council of Thanes. Arman will answer questions about the dwarven kingdoms to the best of his ability. As son of Thane Hornfel, leader of the Hylar, he knows much of the rivalry that plagues the kingdoms of Thorbardin (especially between the Hylar and the Theiwar). At every occasion, he talks about his supposed descent from the dwarven hero Kharas.

If the heroes depart Northgate without Arman, they must find out what to do and where to go by themselves. Most of the possible encounters in this region of Thorbardin are with Theiwar dwarves, who try to lure unwary adventurers into a trap. If the heroes reach the West Warrens, they encounter numerous Hylar farmers, who call for guards to capture the intruders. The guards imprison any captured heroes for 24 hours, then bring them before the Council of Thanes in the Hylar city.

The party departs Northgate either on the First Road of Thanes (if they left Northgate from the lower level) or on the Second Road of Thanes (if they left from the middle level).

10. the First Road of Thanes

> A wide tunnel through the mountain leads into darkness. Metal tracks in the center of the tunnel are twisted and broken. The stone floor is worn smooth. Once, thousands of dwarves must have walked here. Now, there is only dust and emptiness. Your footsteps echo hollowly in the deserted corridor.

The Roads of the Thanes are the major highways that connect the cities and outposts of Thorbardin. In the civilized areas of the realm, small cars roll along the metal tracks, pulled by cables connected to dwarven engines. Carts pulled by beasts of burden travel along the roads, as do dwarves on foot.

The First Road leads to the lower level of the North Hall of Justice.

11. the Second Road of Thanes

This is identical to the First Road, except it leads to the middle level of the North Hall of Justice.

12. the North hall of Justice

The North Hall of Justice (see map) is a small complex of City Blocks that once served as government offices and a second line of defense. When Thorbardin was sealed off from the outside world, the North Hall of Justice fell into disuse. It is now occupied by Theiwar, who prey on unwary travelers.

Sentries are posted in the Great Hall on levels 1 and 2. A party of 40 Theiwar wearing leather armor and carrying light crossbows with poison arrows (see **Monster Manual II**) is stationed in each Kings Gate Block in the complex, where they can fire on intruders through arrow slits in the Kings Wall. All Theiwar are of the lowest type. Arman knows nothing of their presence; he came to Northgate by a different and more dangerous route.

If the party inflicts more than 50% casualties on the Theiwar, the remaining fighters flee. They are not interested in prey that fights back. Arman and his warriors help the heroes.

An additional 250 Theiwar led by a 7-HD Derro Savant and a 6-HD Student Savant live on the upper level. They only attack if the party ventures upstairs.

The First Road of Thanes (lower level) leads on toward the Hylar regions. The Second Road of Thanes leads northeast to the city of the Theiwar. Arman insists on traveling the First Road. If the party should depart the North Hall of Justice on the Second Road, they encounter a war party of 1d10 Theiwar led by a 5-HD commander after 1d4 turns. Each 1d4 turns thereafter, they encounter another party, each with 1d6 more Theiwar than the previous one, until they turn back, are killed, or are captured.

13. Road to the West Warrens

> After many long hours of travel, the Road of the Thanes opens up into a large, natural cavern. The cavern teems with life—huge mushrooms, strange fungi, and other strange plants.

This area is called the West Warrens. The northern section, where the characters enter, is a wilderness. Much of the land in the Warrens is under cultivation: farmers from several of the dwarven kingdoms raise food here.

14. The West Warrens

> The wilderness of fungi gives way to greater order. Here are fields of mushrooms, carefully fenced in. Dwarven farmers labor in the fields. Carts full of mushrooms and fungi, pulled by stunted ponies, travel on dirt roads heading south.

Four shriekers are located at the northern edge of the farms, and begin to cry out when the party approaches. A patrol of 40 Hylar soldiers, wearing chain mail and carrying war hammers, arrives in 1d6 rounds. Their leader calls for the party to stop and identify themselves. If Arman Kharas is with the party, the guards behave with deference, and offer to escort the party to their destination. If the heroes are without Arman Kharas, the guard leader orders them to surrender their weapons. If they refuse, the guards attack, and are joined by an additional 1d10 guards every 5 melee rounds until the party surrenders, is captured, or is killed.

If the characters are captured, they are held in the prisoner block in the Guardian Halls for 24 hours before being brought to the Council of Thanes.

15. Guardian Halls

The Guardian Halls (see map) control passage through the dwarven realms. The Gate Blocks at either side are normally open, but can be shut in case of invasion. Guards in the block check the right of people to pass. A large dungeon holds those who are caught crossing into the wrong kingdom.

If the heroes were captured in the farms, they spend 24 hours in one of the prison cells, and then the guards take them to the city of the Hylar. If the heroes are with Arman Kharas, they pass through the Guardian Hall without incident.

16. The Sixth Road of Thanes

This dwarven highway is in working order. An endless chain of cars travels along the metal tracks, pulled by a strange dwarven engine.

Either in chains or in the company of Arman Kharas, the characters board a car, and are pulled slowly along the road. The ride lasts about half an hour.

17. Docks

The ride ends at one of the Hylar wharfs (see map). The wharfs look out onto the Urkhan Sea, and reveal an amazing sight: the Life-Tree of the Hylar.

The Life-Tree is truly one of the wonders of the world. It is an immense stalactite, half a mile high and as wide at the top, inside which an entire city has been carved (see map).

The city can be reached only by cable-boats (another dwarven invention). The cable-boat leads to Level 1 of the Life-Tree.

If the characters should commandeer a boat and try to visit any of the other cities that line the Urkhan Sea, they are attacked by a dragon turtle.

18. The Life-Tree of the Hylar

A working transport shaft provides passage up the Life-Tree. Hundreds of Hylar dwarves clog the shafts. Most of them have never seen a non-dwarf before, and gawk as the strangers pass. Young children make rude remarks. Riding the transport shaft is quite safe, though the characters may feel otherwise as they look down the long shaft.

The dwarven city is illuminated by a species of glowing coral that works like a **continual light** spell.

If the characters are currently prisoners, they are taken to another dungeon block on level 17 of the city (area "C"). If the characters are with Arman Kharas, they are taken to a place of honor: a well-appointed inn (area "B") on level 28 (the home of the very rich and powerful) in the Kings Gate just outside the Court of Thanes (area "A").

If the characters are free, they can wander around the dwarven city while waiting for the meeting of the Council of Thanes on the following morning.

19. Audience With the Council of the Thanes

The Council of Thanes rules Thorbardin. Each of the nine dwarven kingdoms is theoretically entitled to an equal seat on the council. In practice, this is not the case. The Neidar (Hill) Dwarves split with the dwarves of Thorbardin during the Dwarfgate Wars, and so their seat is empty. The seat of the Kingdom of the Dead is quite vacant. The Kingdom of the High King has been vacant for over 300 years—since the time of Derkin. The **NPC Capsules** of the thanes of Thorbardin provide some background on the six thanes that are present.

The Thanes are: Hornfel (Hylar), Bluph (Aghar), Gneiss (Daewar), Realgar (Theiwar), Rance (Daergar), and Tufa (Klar). Hornfel is the father of Arman Kharas, and is sympathetic to the heroes' plight. Realgar is an agent of Verminaard, and sees this as an opportunity to have the derro rule Thorbardin.

To run the Council meeting, first have Arman Kharas (if present) introduce the heroes to the Council and introduce the Thanes to the heroes. Then have the heroes present their case and make their request. Hornfel listens with interest, but Realgar begins to speak with hatred about the hill dwarves and men that brought on the Cataclysm and the Dwarfgate Wars.

Have each player make an Intelligence Check at -5 to intelligence. Any who succeed feel that Realgar's speech patterns are very similar to those of Verminaard. In fact, Realgar is being telepathically controlled by the dragon highmaster.

During Realgar's tirade, tell the players that the derro thane seems to be swaying the Council against them. Finally, the discussion is finished, and the characters are asked to leave the room so that the Council can make its decision.

The Council's debate lasts an hour, then the heroes are invited back in. Hornfel speaks.

> "It is true that you humans brought the Cataclysm upon the world, and it is true that the Neidar made war on Thorbardin. But dark times are here again, and ancient grudges must not control our destiny.
>
> "Here, then, is the decision of the Council—that whosoever recovers the Hammer of Kharas, that person will the dwarves of Thorbardin befriend. If you agree to our terms, and bring the Hammer to us, then may your people pass.
>
> "There is one other condition: that one of your party remain here as a hostage for your safe return."

Life-Tree of the Hylar

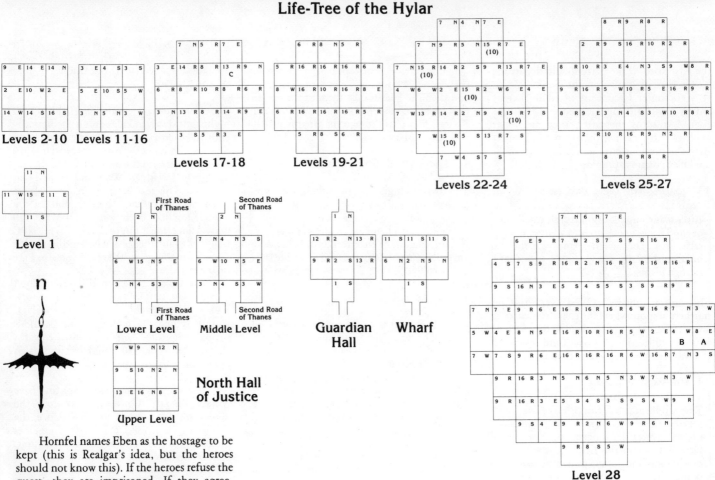

Levels 2-10   Levels 11-16

Levels 17-18

Levels 19-21

Levels 22-24

Levels 25-27

Level 1

n

First Road of Thanes — Second Road of Thanes

Lower Level   Middle Level   Guardian Hall   Wharf

North Hall of Justice

Upper Level

Level 28

Hornfel names Eben as the hostage to be kept (this is Realgar's idea, but the heroes should not know this). If the heroes refuse the quest, they are imprisoned. If they agree, Hornfel tells them that the Hammer lies somewhere in the Valley of Thanes, burial ground of the dwarves. If the heroes have the *Helm of Grallen*, Hornfel thanks them for its return, and asks them to take it to the Valley of Thanes and leave it in the Tomb of Kharas. He tells them that the *Helm* will be of help to them in their quest.

Hornfel raises his hand, and two dwarves enter the chamber. One carries a drum, and one a scroll. They chant the "Song of Kharas."

20. Leaving the kingdom of the hylar

If the heroes do not agree to the quest, they are imprisoned in the dungeon on level 17 of the Life-Tree, and left to rot.

If they agree, Arman begs his father to allow him to accompany the heroes. Hornfel agrees. Arman and a party of Hylar guards escort the heroes away. Eben stays behind as a hostage.

The trip out of the Hylar city is the same as the journey in. The party takes a cable car across the Urkhan Sea to the Eighth Road of Thanes. The trip down the Eighth Road is also by car. The journey ends several hours later at the Guardian Hall complex that opens up onto the Valley of the Thanes—where all the dead of Thorbardin are buried...

The Song of Kharas

Three were the thoughts of those in Thorbardin
In the dark after Dergoth when the ogres danced.
One was the lost light, the limping darkness
In the caves of the kingdom where light crumbles.
One the despair of the Dwarfthane Derkin
Gone to the gloom of the tower of Glory.
One the world, weary and wounded
Down to the deep of the Darkling's waters.
    Under the heart of the highland,
        Under the ceiling of stone,
    Under the wane of the world's glory,
        Home under home.

Then was Kharas among us, the Keeper of Kings,
The Hand on the Hammer, Arm of the Hylar.
At the gleaming gravesite of gold and garnet
Three sons of the thane he buried thereunder.
While Derkin saw dark upon dark in the tunnels,
In the halls of the nation saw nooses and knives,
Killers and kingmakers came to Kharas
With agate and amethyst, asking allegiance.
    Under the heart of the highland,
        Under the ceiling of stone,
    Under the wane of the world's glory,
        Home under home.

But the stalwart in heart is strong as a stone,
And bold and unbending his mind to the better:
The Hammer of Hylar was firm in the halls,
Denying all discord, all doubt and division,
He turned from intrigue, from the wild tunnels,
Out to the open, one oath swearing
That time nor treachery shall ever tarnish
The Hammer's return in a time of great troubles.
    Under the heart of the highland,
        Under the ceiling of stone,
    Under the wane of the world's glory,
        Home under home.

The final kingdom of the dwarves is *Kalil S'rith*, the Valley of Thanes. Here are buried the dwarven dead. Those of royal lineage are entombed in cairns; commoners are interred in humble graves in the stony plain.

If the heroes possess the *Helm of Grallen*, the wearer of the Helm becomes aware that he has the power to turn undead as if a 12th level cleric.

Encounters

21. The Valley of Thanes

> The sun seems a strange sight after many hours in darkness. Ahead lies a dreary, barren valley between the soaring mountains. Everywhere, desolate mounds in the naked earth form burial cairns. Far away, in the heart of the valley, there is a small patch of green—and rising from it, forming a stony pinnacle, is an awesome tomb. The wind whines about the hillocks, seeming to carry the groans and laments of dying warriors. A freezing rain begins, soaking the ground and limiting vision to 100 yards.

22. Tombmounds of the Thanes

> Carven tombs, pitted and worn, replace the simpler cairns. The wind and rain raise a mournful howl.

a. Tomb of Rathkar

> A rotting figure limps down from a large tomb. Its arms are outstretched and it is mumbling. Behind it trail dwarven undead.

This is the mummy of Rathkar, who cannot rest until forgiven by 77 men who listen to his entire life story. He has been forgiven by 31 so far. Rathkar's story takes hours to tell, and he mumbles. His "terrible" sin was that he never told his wife that he loved her.

If the party does not listen or refuses to forgive, Rathkar attacks. He commands 21 skeletons and 19 ghasts. None of the undead can leave this hex, and can be turned only as if 2 levels higher than normal. If destroyed, Rathkar regenerates, but this takes seven years.

B. Spectral Tomb

The undead here hate all life and attack to destroy all intruders. One spectre, two mummies, and eight ghasts are present. They can leave the mound for one turn only, and then are teleported back to their graves for the rest of the day.

23. The Garden

A green oasis surrounds a lake at the valley's center. Stone tombs, covered with ice from the freezing rain, fill the oasis. As soon as the heroes enter the oasis, the rain ends and the sun comes out. Overhead, looming above the lake, is a giant floating rock crowned with a castle—the Tomb of Derkin.

One tomb stands empty before the heroes. On the opposite shore of the lake is a ruin.

a. Tomb of Grallen

Regardless from which direction they approach, Grallen's Tomb stands before the heroes. A 15-foot obelisk stands on the lakeshore. Behind it is a statue of an armored dwarf, arms spread, bare head thrown back. There are Hylar carvings that read: "Raised to honor Prince Grallen, hero of the final assault on the fortress of Fistandantilus."

If the players have the *Helm of Grallen*, it speaks to its wearer, saying, "Bless you, for my brow has been cold these long winters."

When placed on the statue, the helm turns to stone and the statue speaks. "What you seek is above. Its only entrance is across the lake. Say 'I mourn for Kharas' and step through the unbroken arch." The statue then crumbles. If the heroes keep the helm, the wearer must make a save vs. magic once per turn or throw the helmet to the ground. The helm, once dropped, vanishes.

B. Broken Gateway

The ruins across the lake are overgrown with lilies, jasmine and snapdragons. The ground is carpeted with petals. In the ruin's center stands an arch broken in the center. Nine fragments are scattered about it.

If the heroes search the area, they find the nine fragments and a stone plaque engraved in Hylar script. It reads, "I wait and watch; he will not return. Alas, I mourn for Kharas."

The heroes must fit together the nine pieces to rebuild the arch. When the pieces are put in place, they magically merge with the stone until the arch is unbroken again. If the heroes do not think to rebuild the arch, Arman suggests that they do so.

Once the arch is rebuilt, it becomes a teleport device leading to Encounter 24. Saying the phrase, "I mourn for Kharas," activates it.

The Floating Tomb

Derkin's Tomb was build before the Cataclysm. Upon his death, Kharas carried Derkin to his final rest, and here Kharas met his own doom.

Shortly thereafter, Evenstar, the gold dragon, arrived in exile to guard the *Hammer of Kharas*. Evenstar, using hidden knowledge, wrenched the tomb from the earth and set it in the sky. He then filled the tomb with magic peril. Yet his magic is not all danger, for Evenstar loves beauty and light and adorned the castle with these things too.

Derkin's Tomb is 400 feet above the ground. It is built in several levels in the rock on which it floats. Sheer cliffs separate the levels.

The tomb has a feeling of age and wonderment about it. Each room is more exquisite than the last. Even the halls and shafts bear fairylike murals. At any moment it seems the beauty will come to life. It frequently does through the magic of Evenstar's *ring of telekinesis*.

Every six turns a muted gong sounds throughout the tomb.

How to Run This Encounter

The tomb has only one occupant: Evenstar. He uses his spells and abilities to challenge the heroes. To play this section, first review the rules about dragons in **Monster Manual I**, the

description of Evenstar in **NPC Capsules**, and the map of the Floating Tomb on the inside cover. Suggested uses for Evenstar's spells are noted in the encounters below.

Evenstar casts *Guards & Wards* as soon as the heroes enter the tomb, causing:

All doors are *wizard locked*.
Corridors fill with a misty violet vapor that reduces sight to 10 feet.
Inner stairwells, the Spiral Way, and the Elevator shaft fill with *webs*.
Eight doors (random) are hidden behind an illusionary wall. They can only be found by touch.
Every time the heroes choose a direction, they may (50%) move opposite the way they think they are moving.
Everything radiates magic.

Evenstar is basically a peaceful, though world-weary dragon, amused at the heroes' struggle. He enjoys confusing people by changing shape when not observed. He does not reveal that he is a gold dragon until noted in the text, only that he is the guardian of the tomb. He does not use his powers to cause death.

If a hero falls down the shaft or off the tomb, he makes a Dexterity Check at -4 to dexterity to catch himself, or takes 1d6 points of damage for each level fallen. At the bottom of the shaft there is a net that will break the fall, but at 2d6 points of damage. If a character falls off the tomb and does not catch himself, he falls to the lake below, resulting in a total of 10d6 damage (water cushions the fall).

24. Reception Tower

A duplicate of the teleport arch from below is here. As the last hero exits from the teleport, there is a flash of light and the arch vanishes behind them. There is a trapdoor in the roof, but no ladder to the floor below.

25. Lower Gallery & Stairs

This wooden walk is weakened in several places. There is a 10% chance it breaks. Each character must make a Dexterity Check or fall 10 feet.

Evenstar can cast *push* on a hero climbing the stairs, causing him to topple back into the others. This causes all affected heroes to take 1d6 damage.

26. Hall of Enemies

The booty of victory, the weapons, armor and shield of Derkin's defeated enemies, is stored here. Evenstar may use his *ring of telekinesis* to make things appear to move.

27. Upper Galleries

This is a stone walkway. At the top of the stairs a voice (*magic mouth*) cries out in Hylar, "Defilers, begone! Tempt not the sleep of the ageless." The passage slopes upward to the north past several archways.

Evenstar can cast *rock to mud* and *dancing lights*.

28. Votive Cells

These are bare, stone cells.

29. Overlook

From this overlook, to the east lie the ruins. In the distance to the west is another exit from the valley. South are the nests of giant vultures in the caves. To the north, the snow-shrouded peaks of the mountains are covered by a huge army crawling down into the valley. The enemy is coming. (This sight can be seen from every overlook in the tomb.)

30. Fountain of Time

In the center of this room is a moss-covered fountain. Lying against the fountain is a white-bearded sleeping dwarf. He meets the general description of Kharas. This is Evenstar. If the heroes awaken him, he appears dazed. He has trouble understanding that time has passed or where his hammer has gone. He had stopped for a drink after burying Derkin and that's all he remembers. (If any heroes drink from the fountain, roll dice as if checking for an effect, then look relieved and say that they made it.) "Kharas" agrees to go with the heroes. After Encounter 36 he slips away or changes form.

31. Antechamber

These walls are marbled and mirrored, making the room seem larger.

32. Banquet Hall

Long tables are lined with fine foods. Fruits and sweets are spread in the center of the tables. The room is filled with the aroma of good cooking.

Upon closer examination, the food is found to be made of precious metal, gems, and jewels, worth thousands of stl. Making the best choices, each person might be able to take 2,000 stl worth. "Kharas" warns against theft here.

In the center of the room is a tall chair, a reading table, and a book. Lying on the book is a pair of ruby-colored spectacles. The book is a history of Derkin, written in an obscure tongue.

The spectacles have the following properties: *infravision, ultravision, comprehend languages,* and *read magic.* They also act as a *gem of seeing.* They can be worn for up to four hours a day without ill effects. If worn longer, they give the wearer a splitting headache (-4 to THAC0).

33. Grand Overlook

See Encounter 29 for what can be seen. The floor here is rotten; there is a 10% chance per 50 pounds that a character falls through. Falling characters make a Dexterity Check to catch themselves; failure results in a 20 foot drop to the support beams below for 3d6 of damage.

34. Grand Promenade

This corridor is lined with shallow niches holding granite statues of noble dwarves.

Evenstar can cast *stinking cloud* in this area.

35. Tipping Path

See the diagram on the map. This bridge is lined with crossbars supported by a central metal beam. When the party crosses the bridge, it flips over once more than half the total party weight crosses the midpoint. Characters may catch hold of a crossbar by making a successful Dexterity Check, or fall down the shaft.

36. Elevator Shaft

This is a square shaft filled with *webs.* A cascade of ice chips fall from the shaft and evaporate as they strike the floor.

37. Ruby Tower of Singing Light

The room at the tower's base holds crystals and colored glass bits. From above comes the sound of heavenly chimes. The tower itself is flooded with a rainbow of light dancing on the walls and crystal chimes ringing in the wind.

38. Shrine of Reorx the Forge

On the altar are three items and a tapestry that reads, "Take you in need." Any who enter the shrine are filled with a feeling of anticipated battle. The three items are a potion of *extra healing,* a scroll of *remove curse* and *prayer,* and a necklace with three *prayer beads—bless, cure,* and *karma.* Evenstar can identify the beads.

39 - 41. Histories of Derkin

These three chambers tell the story of Derkin's life, creations and battles through dioramas and trophies. They include his triumph over Bonecrusher the Ogre and his final battle fought atop Mt. Skull. Evenstar may use his *ring of telekinesis* to make things come to life or use *dancing lights* to lure party members to the elevator shaft.

42. Unseen Danger

This room is filled with red light from the level above. A pendulum swings 30 feet overhead. It is a hammer. This room has a red glass partial floor that is invisible in the light of the tower. It appears that the room opens onto the shaft. The real floor is a network with gaps. Invisible, overhead swinging logs strike at (THAC0 15) anything above 3 feet tall. On the far side of the room is a brass ladder leading up.

43. Courtyard

From this flagstone courtyard, the heroes can see sights as described in Encounter 29. The cap of the large ruby tower bears a sharp spike. In the center of the courtyard beside a hole lies a 16-foot flagpole with a lance tip. This is a crude model of the dragonlance. An inscription on the wall of the Pilgrim's Hostel (Encounter 44) reads:

> lances did great Huma seek
> To forge upon the dragon's peak
> With silver arm and silver pool
> And Hammer would he forge wyrms' doom.

44. Pilgrim's Hostel

This is a refuge for visiting pilgrims. A ramp circles a fountain, providing two tiers of stone cells. Here is the gear and *plate mail +1* of Kharas.

45. Lonely Vigil

This tower is dark. A set of stairs spiral up around a water-filled cistern to a balcony. The stairs are covered with webs and broken in several places. An uncautious hero may fall 10-30 feet.

Evenstar may use *phantasmal force* to make the cistern appear to release a flood of water for 3d4 damage.

At the top of the tower is a wooden cylinder containing a magic scroll with *flame arrow, fire shield* and *haste.*

46. Dilemma

In this tower is a gushing fountain. A ramp leads downward. The room is 30 feet high, the fountain spouting nearly to the ceiling. If a player decides to look closely, have him make an Intelligence Check. If he is successful, he sees a small wooden platform bobbing at the top of the fountain. This platform has a permanent *levitate* spell cast on it, but can only support 20 pounds. On the platform is a potion of *superheroism* and a wand of *frost* with only 3 charges left. The command word ("O.G.") is written in runes on the wand.

47. Vestibule

This room is filled with an obscuring smoke which will slowly dissipate once the door is opened. A broken phial lies on the floor.

On the floor before the second set of doors is the corpse of a dwarf. He wears the signet ring of Kharas. This is the true Kharas. If Evenstar is masquerading as Kharas he admits that he is just the guardian of the tomb and has been testing them. He does not change into a dragon.

Beneath Kharas' heel are the remains of a small scorpion; he was ignobly stung to death. A stone phial attached to his belt contains a fluid which forms an obscuring cloud of smoke, 40 feet by 40 feet by 20 feet, when poured on the ground.

48. Ruby Chamber of the Hammer

The room is hot, lit with a sanguine light streaming through crimson windows. Only a narrow balcony thrusts over the shaft that opens to the distant lake below.

Hanging from a slender thread, a mighty bronze hammer swings back and forth. Every hour it strikes one of the gongs thrusting out from the walls.

Evenstar casts an invisible cylindrical *wall of force* over the swinging Hammer. The Hammer may then only be retrieved by finding some way to sever the cord and catch it; climb beneath and up to it, or by waiting for the end of the spell.

Using a crystal and mirror or the ruby glasses to focus the sunlight burns the cord through and the Hammer falls to the invisible floor below room 42.

49. Watch Tower

This three-story tower contains two ballistae and ammunition. Bunks, kegs of oil, and a gong are above. A wooden ladder leads up to the steeple.

50. Test of Determination

Wind fills this room, moaning up from the shaft. Swaying in the wind across this pit is the remnant of a rope bridge. Now only a single strand remains with several boards still attached. A hand-over-hand crossing requires three Dexterity checks. To tightrope walk, make two checks at +4 penalty or -20% for thief Climb Walls.

51. Robber's Trap

A fountain of flame is in the center of this room. Set in the wall is a buttressed stone gate with a lever.

This room is trapped to dispose of robbers. The trap is activated by pushing up on the lever, or by removing the stone pin which stops the lever from moving down. When activated a block of stone drops across the entrance and the ceiling begins to drop, causing the flame to fan out. It drops to head height in 5 rounds and then descend one foot per round, spreading the flame one foot each round. It stops two feet above the floor, and then resets in 2 rounds. The flame causes 2d6 points of damage. The stone valve is only a false door. The exit from this room is a concealed sliding stone panel.

52. Derkin's Final Peace

This set of stone gates opens by pushing at the bottom. In the center is a bier holding the coffin of Derkin. The lid is carved to resemble Derkin. In this room are statues of servants and a golden anvil that weighs 8,000 gp. Several chests hold resplendent garments and furs worth 5,000 steel. On a stand is Derkin's golden *plate mail +3*, helm and shield with the avenging flame. The armor is cursed for any who steal it. It becomes AC 10 at a critical moment in battle. Also here is a two-handed bronze *war axe +2* and a *ring of protection +2*.

Endgame: Raging Ember:

This occurs as the heroes exit the main tower with the Hammer of Kharas. If Evenstar is not with the heroes, he is waiting for them as Kharas. A shadow crosses his face and he looks skyward. There on the tower's cap perches Ember, the red dragon. Verminaard is not astride Ember. Evenstar shakes his head at those who draw weapons.

In a voice that is a hissing roar, Ember speaks, "So Old One, you consort with my enemies! More, you hide behind their puny form! Step aside, they are mine! No man holds back my hand now!"

Evenstar smiles, "Begone child! Do not tempt my anger. Do you desire death so?"

Ember's lips curl in a cruel snarl. "No, Old One! It is you who tempt fate! I know the Oath; by the power of your word you are bound! Not even the terror of the dragonlance could bind one so well. Come, Evenstar, show these puny mortals what company they keep, or has the Council stripped you of your pride too?"

The dwarf's face clouds with anger; his form swells, taking on a golden hue, stretching and growing until there stands a golden dragon. Ember laughs in derision. Evenstar turns to the heroes and tells them Ember is right, he may not interfere.

Ember bellows, "Prepare to die!" and takes flight. Remember the dragon ability to *cause fear*. Ember does not attack Evenstar intentionally. She circles and breathes, then claws and bites as she glides the next two rounds. Then she climbs, banks, and swoops to breathe again. Finally, she dives for double claw damage and then lands to fight and cast spells.

Evenstar does not help unless Ember causes Evenstar damage or she harms either ruby tower. If this happens, Evenstar flies into a rage and attacks.

The Hammer does not use its special abilities. If thrown off the tower, Evenstar has it after the fight.

If the heroes use the flagpole as a heavy lance (Dmg 3-18) to set against Ember's dive, it causes double damage. Ember will be able to avoid the lance if she can see it.

Evenstar suggests that the lance be used if the heroes do not think of it.

Fight's End: When Ember is reduced to 5 or fewer hit points, she screams in a final death cry, takes to the air, tries to fly away, falters, and tumbles backward onto the spike on the tower cap.

Warhorns sound from the valley below. The army approaches. Evenstar collapses and changes to Kharas. He is aging and the tomb trembles. He speaks, "I have completed at last my fateful mission, and now the end is upon me. Take the Hammer—let it not fall into the enemy's hands! Flee east and fail not."

He encourages Arman to guard the Hammer and fulfill his destiny. He gives the heroes six horse statuettes. They are to throw them to the ground and cry "Branchala Guide Me!" The statuettes become living horses for three turns (move 24"), and can be used three times.

As the heroes mount to flee, a raucous screeching is heard. Six young dragons, Ember's brood, are heading for the tomb. The horses rear and then leap off the side of the tomb. Failed Dexterity checks mean the hero is hanging from the saddle. At the last moment the horses *feather fall*.

Behind, the fledglings circle the tower in confusion. The tomb shudders, crumbling, until the spike breaks, tossing Ember's broken form earthward. Then the tomb slowly sinks. The army starts a mile away, but moves a mile a turn. The heroes must flee or be captured.

Exit: As the heroes reach the eastern entrance, shadows glide past as a party of eight Kapak dragonmen drop from the cliff top. From the mouth of the tunnel rides a bozak astride a subterranean lizard.

Events

Event 5: Escape

This Event takes place immediately after the heroes leave Derkin's Tomb.

> As the great tomb crumbles, you see the mass of the approaching dragonarmies giving chase. Your horses gallop away, but your pursuers grow ever closer!

There is a 10% chance per turn that a scouting patrol of 8 baaz draconians come within 10-60 yards of the heroes and charge to the attack.

Remember, the magic steeds only last for three turns, and can be regenerated only twice. Once used up, the heroes must proceed on foot. The dragonarmies have occupied most of the Valley of Thanes. The only clear escape route for the heroes is in the direction of the Guardian Hall leading to the Ninth Road of Thanes.

The Gateway block leading into the Guardian Hall is shattered and torn. The Great Hall block leading to the road is also cracked and broken. Regardless of scouts encountered, the main body of the dragonarmy is ten combat rounds behind the heroes. If not delayed, the army pursues the heroes into the Road of the Thanes. This increases the frequency of random encounters

in these tunnels to one check every two combat rounds.

In describing the Great Hall, note that the roof is supported by pillars that are cracked and fragile. Pulling down a pillar takes a combined strength of 45. If three pillars are pulled down, the ceiling collapses. It takes the dragonarmies six turns to dig through.

Event 6: The Hunt

This region is controlled by the Daergar kingdom, currently allied with the Theiwar and with Verminaard. In addition to normal random encounters, check three times (1 on 1d6) to see if the party encounters a Daergar patrol, consisting of 12 Daergar and 1 shadow mastiff. The patrol always begins 10-60 yards behind the heroes. If encountered, the patrol gives chase. The shadow mastiff bays, requiring a save vs. magic at +9 (see **Monster Manual II**).

If a Daergar patrol attacks, each turn there is a 10% chance that another identical patrol joins the hunt.

Encounters

The South Hall of Justice once served a role similar to that of the North Hall, but is now controlled by the Daergar. It is also occupied by Verminaard and his forces. Once the heroes

have entered the Ninth Road of Thanes from the Guardian Hall, the only route leads to the South Hall. This is a very critical part of the adventure, and must be carefully run.

The enemy forces should be in hot pursuit of the adventurers. Emphasize the urgent nature of their flight from the derro and the dragonarmies. If the heroes are cornered at any point, the enemy will call for them to surrender. If the heroes surrender, they are escorted under heavy guard to the Temple of Stars (Encounter 62). Their weapons are taken from them, but they are not bound.

If the heroes are not captured, they should end up in the Prison (Encounter 53) where they meet Eben and Berem. From there, Eben should urge them to go north to leave this complex. They must enter the Temple of Stars to escape, and there the final scene takes place.

53. Prisoners of the Daergar

As soon as the heroes cross the drawbridge in the King's Wall, they hear terrible cries coming from the next block. The next block is a dwarven prison guarded by 20 Daergar, who are outside the cell area. Once the Daergar are defeated, entering the cell complex is easy.

There are 100 prisoners held here, but only 20 Hylar, 10 Men, and 5 Kender are in shape to fight. The Daergar have weapons to equip all fighters.

Eben is found in one of the cells, along with an old man. Eben is very glad to see the party; he says that after the heroes left on the quest, there was a raid on the Hylar city and he was kidnapped by Daergar. Eben's clothes are torn and he has bruises, but he is not actually hurt. The other prisoners confirm that he was brought into the prison by derro guards, beaten, and thrown into the cell. In fact, Eben is here only to lead the party to Verminaard so that the dragon highmaster can recover the *Hammer of Kharas*. Verminaard arranged Eben's placement here through his puppet Realgar.

Eben says he thinks he can find the way out of the kingdom; he saw the commander's maps. If permitted to guide the party, he leads them to the final encounter in a roundabout fashion.

The old man in Eben's cell has forgotten how to talk and is slow to understand. He has evidently been here for a very long time; his beard and hair are waist-length and his clothes are in tatters. His long beard conceals a strange gem implanted in his chest. This is Berem Everman (see **NPC Capsules**). He follows the party until the next fight. At that time, regardless of dice rolls, he takes an evidently mortal wound and falls to the ground. When the party moves on, one of the heroes looks back and sees Berem stand, look confused, and run off in another direction.

After the prisoners are freed, no enemies appear for ten rounds. The heroes can follow Eben, who claims to know the way out, find another way out, or stand and fight. Verminaard has ordered his forces to capture, not kill, them. If captured, the heroes are brought to the Temple of the Stars (Encounter 62). If the heroes retreat or follow Eben, the enemy forces them in the direction of Encounter 62.

54. Invasion of the Daergar

Enemy troops have entered the South Hall of Justice through the Seventeenth Road of Thanes. Wherever this encounter occurs, a party of 25 derro and 25 baaz draconians led by a kapak draconian riding a subterranean lizard attack the party. Their objective is to capture, not kill, or to force the party into the prison cell block (Encounter 53).

Special Encounters

The following special encounters can take place anywhere in the South Hall complex. You may use some, none, or all of these to help guide the adventure. Normal random encounters can be used in addition to or in spite of these encounters.

55. Warning

Impaled on a staff is a grotesque, tusked skull. There is a 50% chance that there is a spiked spring trap hidden here (2d6 damage).

Each turn after the heroes pass, there is a 10% chance of a *magic mouth* shouting, "Intruder!"

56. Bonemaster

This rogue dwarf has a few assistants gnawing bones clean. He designs weapons, armor, and tools from the bones. He is able to animate bones; there are 20 derro skeletons nearby. He uses others to cover his escape.

57. Goatherd

Here, a group of six Daergar tend their "goatherd" — twenty giant cave crickets grazing on fungi and garbage. Their sudden chirping has a 2 in 6 chance of drawing a random encounter.

58. Curtained Alcove

As the party passes through this block, they see a curtained alcove off to one side. Inside, is a pretty lady, dressed in rags, chained to the wall. She is a lamia noble.

59. Survival of the Fittest

Here, a giant cave beetle and a giant lizard do battle. The heroes can slip by if they move quietly. If there is a commotion, the monsters turn on the party.

60. Petrified Remains

Here are the petrified remains of a mastodon. If the bonemaster (Encounter Area 56) has followed the party, he animates the skeleton, which cannot be turned while the bonemaster is alive. (HD 13, hp52, AC 4, THAC0 8, AT 2d8(x2)/2d6(x2))

the final Battle

This is the climax of the First Book of Dragonlance. Read the following section carefully. Although extremely dangerous, it can be survived if the heroes think and act intelligently. There is a lot of roleplaying here; try to understand the needs and objectives of all the NPCs before beginning play.

61. Doorway to Despair

No matter from which direction the heroes approach the final encounter, they find themselves heading down a strangely familiar corridor...

The way ahead of you dims, as if the light of your torches and lanterns is being sucked up by the grim dwarven halls. The area around you takes on the feeling of a dream, as if you are sleepwalking. An awful feeling of *deja vu* creeps into your soul...for you were here once before, in a dream.

Memories of your nightmare in the Mind of Evil flood back, for the corridor stretching into the next dwarven block is the corridor into your dream!

If characters try to go in another direction, they encounter parties of Daergar and draconians that fight to either capture them or force them into the final encounter.

62. the Final Battle

This encounter takes place in the Temple of Stars (City Block 12). Review the map block carefully to place all the participants in it. In locations 2 and 4, the ceiling has caved in, blocking the passage so that the party must enter the main temple area.

If the party was captured previously, they are brought into this area bound, but the bonds are removed. Their weapons are piled nearby. If the party did not release Eben from the prison, he will be brought in to stand by Verminaard, apparently a prisoner too.

The great hall north is barred by a locked golden gate. Suddenly, the face of Verminaard, ten feet tall, appears in mid-air, and a telepathic voice booms in your heads. "Finally! You are mine!" The doors fling open and nearly two hundred Daergar rush in, weapons at the ready.

Verminaard laughs. "So now you know what lies beyond the doorway of dreams. Nothing can save you now!"

A horn sounds from behind the golden gates and the image fades. The Daergar cower as a light magically shines on the gates. Suddenly, the gates are flung open. A party of four warriors, one a dark-haired woman, four draconians, two ogres, and an ettin, all wearing the uniforms of officers in the army of the dragon highmaster enter. They part, and from behind them strides Verminaard, clothed in black armor. He steps up onto a balcony over the central pit, and laughs with sinister joy. "Welcome to despair!" he shouts.

In addition to all items and spells in Verminaard's **NPC Capsule**, he wears a ring of *pro-*

jection, a ring of *protection vs. normal missiles*, and a *brooch of shielding*. He has cast *resist fire* on himself. If the heroes attempt to attack, he shrugs it off. The Daergar fire a flight of darts to warn the heroes.

If the heroes entered the Mind of Evil, have them review their dream cards and remind them of the details of the dream. Tell them that the room seems to be shifting and changing to become more and more like the dream. Sturm and Laurana feel that this is not where their dreams took place.

Verminaard speaks again. "Word has reached me that Ember has been slain! For that you will surely pay! You thought to best me by gaining the *Hammer of Kharas*, but I was in control all along. I permitted you to retrieve what I could not. Now I have you and the Hammer, and with it I shall command the dwarven kingdoms. To show you how futile has been your struggle, one of your own will bring the Hammer to me."

His gaze sweeps over the party members. Ask each player in turn if he will voluntarily take the Hammer to Verminaard. If all refuse (as they should), Eben Shatterstone reveals himself as the traitor. Take Eben's Character Card back from the player and have Eben tell the party that, indeed, he works for Verminaard. If Eben is not with the party, Verminaard can attempt to telepathically control anyone with a wisdom of 10 or less. The person he attempts to control may make a save vs. spells to resist. If all resist, Verminaard has his personal guard retrieve the Hammer.

At this point, remember the special powers of the *Hammer of Kharas* (see **NPC Capsules & Magic Items**). It can possess its wielder and personally act to make events come out to its satisfaction. Give the players a chance to save themselves; but if they fail, the Hammer can take an active role.

Verminaard laughs as the *Hammer of Kharas* is taken from you. The hammer-wielder says to you, "You are fools to resist my master! He will reward me richly; you will see your folly when I am made governor of this land!"

"Hold your tongue, lackey," snarls Verminaard. "You are simply a pawn, and you will serve your betters! Bring me the Hammer!"

The traitor is outraged, and protests, but Verminaard exerts his will and the unwilling lackey moves closer to giving Verminaard the

Hammer. But as he reaches the dragon highmaster, the Hammer suddenly begins to glow. The Daergar are awed, and kneel. The traitor passes from the influence of Verminaard to the influence of the Hammer.

Verminaard is livid at the disobedience, and demands again that the traitor bring him the weapon. But the traitor is fully under the Hammer's control, and says, "With this hammer, I control the dwarven realms, not you!" He throws the Hammer at Verminaard, automatically hitting for maximum damage. The Hammer rebounds, and lands at the edge of the pit. The Daergar begin to chant the name of the traitor as he bends to pick up the Hammer.

But at that moment, Verminaard casts *spiritual hammer*, hitting the traitor automatically for maximum damage, and keeps him from retrieving the Hammer. Each round thereafter, Verminaard strikes again for maximum damage, slowly crushing the hapless traitor.

Battle Royale

Now, the heroes have a chance to break free. There is one derro for each hero in the party; they must be overcome before the heroes can recover their weapons, if they were captured earlier.

The Daergar soldiers are only concerned with who possesses the Hammer. Its influence keeps them from being active in the battle. If the heroes liberated the prisoners earlier, the prisoners fight an equal number of Daergar. The heroes must defeat Verminaard's guard and the dragon highmaster himself to win.

Once the traitor is dead, Verminaard tears a dragon-headed necklace from around his neck and throws it into the pit, crying, "Come, oh mighty Queen! Send me your servant so that your child may be avenged!" Silence follows, and then from the pit rises a horror—a fireshadow! The fireshadow resembles a wraithlike dragon limned in pale green fire.

The fireshadow first attacks one of the prisoners with its *ray of oblivion*, disintegrating him. Next, it strikes a Daergar, converting him into dark flame. The heroes must defeat the fireshadow and the dark flame Daergar in addition to their other foes.

If the heroes do not think to retrieve the Hammer and use it against the fireshadow, it glows and rings out. The Hammer only allows Eben, Arman, Tasslehoff, Flint, or Caramon to pick it up. The fireshadow automatically attacks any person holding the Hammer. The Hammer can dispel the fireshadow if it hits the creature. The Hammer arcs through the

monster and it fades away, but then the Hammer falls at Verminaard's feet.

If the heroes entered the Mind of Evil and had their dream, suddenly they sense the mind of Elistan among them. Hope floods into their souls, and they are +2 to hit and -2 to AC for the remainder of this battle. Verminaard staggers back under the mind of Elistan, and is -2 to hit and +2 to AC hereafter.

Verminaard, reeling, stoops to pick up the Hammer. "You may think you have won, but this battle is not yet over!" he cries. But when he lifts the Hammer, he cries out in pain and takes 15 points of damage. He cannot hold the Hammer and flings it away. Verminaard continues to fight, but when he is down to his last few hit points, he says, "You shall not have the satisfaction of taking me alive," wraps his cloak around him, and steps into the pit, falling to his death without a sound.

Once Verminaard is dead, the Daergar flee and Verminaard's guard is -1 to hit, damage, and save.

Death of a Hero

Regardless of actual battle events, Arman Kharas takes a fatal wound in this fight. As the final enemies flee or die, a faint whisper is heard from the crumpled form of Arman. There is no saving him; he seems to have been poisoned.

If the heroes attempt to aid him, he shakes his head and says, "No, I am undone. No aid will save me. Take the hammer to my father; he will unify the kingdom. Tell him not to mourn, I have served the Wheel well. I know I am not Kharas, but I have driven the darkness back."

And with his final words, he dies.

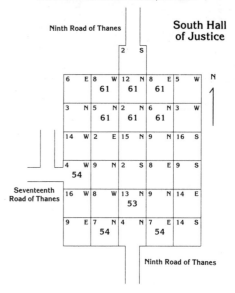

canticle of the dragon

Out of the darkness of dragons,
out of our cries for light
in the blank face of the black moon soaring,
a banked light flared in Solamnia,
a knight of truth and of power,
who called down the gods themselves
and forged the mighty Dragonlance, piercing the soul
of dragonkind, driving the shade of their wings
from the brightening shores of Krynn.

Paladine, the Great God of Good
shone at the side of Huma,
strengthening the lance of his strong right arm,
and Huma, ablaze in a thousand moons,
banished the Queen of Darkness,
banished the swarm of her shrieking hosts
back to the senseless kingdom of death, where their curses
swooped upon nothing and nothing
deep below the brightening land.

Thus ended in thunder the Age of Dreams
and began the Age of Might,
When Istar, kingdom of light and truth, arose in the east,
where minarets of white and gold
spired to the sun and to the sun's glory,
announcing the passing of evil,
and Istar, who mothered and cradled the long summers of good,
shone like a meteor
in the white skies of the just.

Yet in the fullness of sunlight
the Kingpriest of Istar saw shadows:
At night he saw the trees as things with daggers, the streams
blackened and thickened under the silent moon.
He searched books for the paths of Huma
for scrolls, signs, and spells
so that he, too, might summon the gods, might find
their aid in his holy aims,
might purge the world of sin.

Then came the time of dark and death
as the gods turned from the world.
A mountain of fire crashed like a comet through Istar,
the city split like a skull in the flames,
mountains burst from once-fertile valleys,
seas poured into the graves of mountains,
the deserts sighed on abandoned floors of the seas,
the highways of Krynn erupted
and became the paths of the dead.

Thus began the Age of Despair.
The roads were tangled.
The winds and the sandstorms dwelt in the husks of cities,
The plains and mountains became our home.
As the old gods lost their power,
we called to the blank sky
into the cold, dividing gray to the ears of new gods.
The sky is calm, silent, unmoving.
We had yet to hear their answer.

Then to the east, to the Sunken City
scarred in its loss of blue light,
came the Heroes, the Innfellows, heirs to the burdens,
out of their tunnels and their arching forests,
out of the lowness of plains, the lowness
of huts in the valleys,
the stunned farms under the warlords and darkness.
They came serving the light,
the covered flames of healing and grace.

From there, pursued by the armies,
the cold and glittering legions, they came
bearing the staff to the arms of the shattered city,
where below the weeds and the birdcall,
below the vallenwood, below forever,
below the riding darkness itself,
a hole in the darkness called to the source of the light,
drawing all light to the core of light,
to the first fullness of its godly dazzle.

Endgame

If the heroes fail to defeat Verminaard in the final battle, then the forces of dark and of the dragon highmaster triumph. The heroes almost certainly are captured. The *Hammer of Kharas* falls into the hands of evil, and the Theiwar thane takes the throne of Thorbardin. The forces of evil prevail. This concludes the adventure in darkness — though the heroes may yet escape to fight again.

If the heroes defeat Verminaard and recover the *Hammer of Kharas*, a party of Hylar dwarves led by Hornfel Kytil arrives shortly after Arman Kharas' death. He asks the heroes to give him the Hammer.

If the heroes give Hornfel the *Hammer of Kharas*, he hails them as saviors of Thorbardin, and grants them and all their companions safe passage through the kingdom. Each character who survived is made an honorary War Leader (equivalent to a knighthood), and a citizen of Thorbardin. If the heroes refuse, the Hammer uses its powers to take over its wielder, and gives itself into the hands of Hornfel. Hornfel treats the heroes the same as if they gave him the Hammer voluntarily.

It is vital that the Hammer end up in the hands of Hornfel, for it is the only device that can forge the Dragonlances. The players, of course, should not learn this until much later.

Possession of the *Hammer of Kharas* allows Hornfel to declare himself King of Thorbardin. As King, he can assert authority over the Theiwar and Daergar, and once again open Thorbardin to the outside world.

Rescue of the Refugees

At this point, determine how much time remains before the dragonarmies reach the refugee camp. Ask the players whether they want to travel quickly or slowly back to the camp. Quick travel takes one day from the South Hall; slow travel takes two days. Do not tell the players how much time is left!

If the heroes return too late...

A vision out of nightmare greets you as you approach the refugee camp. For where there were once 800 living souls, now there is only death and destruction. Men, women, and children are strewn about like rag dolls. The wagons are smashed; the fragile lean-tos are burned. Mixed with the refugees are the remains of draconians—the defenders of the camp fought bravely to the end and took many enemies with them.

You returned too late. The dragonarmies have won yet another victory. Your quest to find safety for these people has been for naught…but the battle for Krynn is not yet over!

While in dragonarmy-occupied territory, the characters have an encounter with eight baaz draconians once every four game turns in addition to normal random encounters.

Twenty refugees led by Laurana managed to escape, carrying the body of Elistan. They make their way to Northgate, and are found there. Elistan revived shortly after the heroes defeated Verminaard, and has told the story of the final battle to the survivors.

Continue with the final scene below—but the final feast is dimmed with sorrow, and the ending of this saga is not a happy one. Instead of remaining at Southgate, the few remaining refugees elect to accompany the heroes south to Tarsis.

Because the players failed in their mission, they lose 50% of the experience points they earned in this adventure.

If the Heroes Return in Time...

> As you approach the refugee camp, a mighty cheer goes up. The survivors of Pax Tharkas are happier than they have been in many a day. Men, women, and children rush to greet you...and at their head is Elistan, risen again.
>
> Elistan lifts his hand, and the people fall silent. "Welcome!" he cries, and another great cheer erupts from the crowd.
>
> "We must leave quickly, ere the dragonarmies reach our camp. But now that you are here, we know that safety and freedom are not far away."

As the refugees quickly pack their few belongings, Elistan takes the heroes aside. If the heroes entered the Mind of Evil in Chapter 14, Elistan says, "Thank you for bringing hope into the Mind of Evil. Thanks to you, I was able to stave off the dark forces and attack Verminaard at the critical moment. I witnessed your final battle, then awoke at the death of Verminaard to bring news of your victory to the people. We have awaited your coming, and now know that freedom is in our grasp."

If the heroes did not enter the Mind of Evil, Elistan says, "I was consumed by the darkness of Verminaard. My strength and faith were barely enough to keep me free. But Verminaard's death freed me, and I awoke to bring news of your victory to our people. We have awaited your coming, and now know that freedom is at last in our grasp."

Passage Through Thorbardin

The survivors of the eight hundred refugees follow the characters into Northgate, and through the long halls of the dwarven kingdom to its southern exit: Southgate. (For mapping purposes, Southgate is identical to Northgate except for the compass direction.)

Hornfel, now wearing the crown of the high king, comes to Southgate to welcome the refugees. "We greet you, the first humans to pass through our kingdom in many centuries. For the courage of your leaders, and for their contribution to at last reuniting the dwarves of Thorbardin, we are pleased to grant you the land outside the Southgate as a refuge until darkness lifts from Krynn."

The land is able to support the surviving refugees, and it will be a long time before the dragonarmies reunite under another leader. For the time being, the refugees are safe. The Council of Freedom elects to remain here, while the heroes, accompanied by Elistan, go south to the seaport of Tarsis to arrange passage for the refugees to lands free of the menace—if, indeed, such lands exist.

The characters should remain with the refugees for a few weeks, to recover from their trials and receive the level advancements they have earned by training with dwarven masters and rescued veterans.

If the characters saved the refugees, they each receive a bonus of 1,000 experience points in addition to any other points earned in the adventure.

The heroes have several meetings with Hornfel, and attend the funeral of Arman Kharas. The dwarves gladly furnish the heroes with whatever supplies and equipment (no magical items) they need for their quest southward.

During this period, Riverwind and Goldmoon decide to marry. This is the occasion for a great feast—the final event of this story...

The Wedding of Goldmoon and Riverwind

> Autumn warmth fills the glade of trees. Behind you, the shadow of the great mountain looms. The huge dwarven gate is open, a sign of safety and refuge.
>
> Everywhere there is peace and rejoicing. Children and parents alike dance in the glade's soft grasses. Music fills the air. The sunset is impossibly rich and brilliant.
>
> It is a time of peace and rejoicing, for this is the marriage of Goldmoon and Riverwind. Celebration is in the air. And, as the sun sets, a line of dwarves, carrying torches, winds its way down from Southgate to attend the feast. Elistan calls the people together...

The Wedding Song, presented on the next page, was written for the feast of this marriage. You can perform it or read it aloud. Elistan conducts the wedding service, and when the two are joined, shouts of jubilation are everywhere. The feast lasts long into the night. And late, around the campfire, the Canticle may once again be recited.

The Story Ends

> Late at night, you join your companions on a ridge, looking south. The plains of Tarsis stretch to the flat horizon. Somewhere to the south the shining city of Tarsis stands; somewhere its towers gleam in the sunshine, and its ships set sail for lands free of tyranny.
>
> Verminaard is dead, but soon another dragon highlord will arise to take his place. The first battle has been won, but the war continues.
>
> Perhaps in Tarsis answers can be found. Why have dragons returned to Krynn? What is the power of the dragon highmasters? How can they be defeated?
>
> And somewhere in the world is the key to the Dragonlances—for if the Hammer of Kharas was no myth, then the Dragonlances may also exist. If they can be found, perhaps the tide can be turned, and you can take back the stolen northlands.

Here ends the First Book of DRAGONLANCE™. Knowledge of the true gods has returned to troubled Krynn, and with knowledge, hope.

The Second Book of DRAGONLANCE tells of the heroes' role in the Great War, and of the discovery of the great lances. Many mysteries are revealed, and new ones arise.

In the Third Book of DRAGONLANCE, the saga concludes by showing how the will of one man can change the fate of the world—for good or ill—and reveals the final mysteries and fate of the dragons of Krynn.

The

DragonLance™

Design Team

Tracy Hickman, Series Concept

Harold Johnson, Director of Design

Margaret Weis	Douglas Niles
J. Jeffrey Grubb	Michael Dobson
Larry Elmore	Elizabeth Riedel
Bruce Nesmith	Carl Smith
Garry Spiegle	Roger Moore
Laura Hickman	

Verminaard, Dragon Highlord of the Red Wing

Eighth Level Lawful Evil Cleric

Strength 14	Dexterity 10
Intelligence 12	Constitution 15
Wisdom 16	Charisma 18
THAC0 16	Hit Points 50
Armor Class 1	Movement 12″

Spells:

Level 1: *cause fear, cause light wounds (x2), command (x2), darkness*
Level 2: *hold person (x2), resist fire, silence 15 ft. radius, spiritual hammer (x2)*
Level 3: *cause blindness, dispel magic, prayer*
Level 4: *cause serious wounds (x2)*

Wears *plate mail +2*. Carries *Nightbringer mace +2*. On a successful hit, victim must save vs. spells or be blinded for 2-12 turns (-4 to AC, lose shield and dexterity bonus to AC). If character of good alignment tries to hold it, must save vs. spells at -2 or be permanently blinded.

Verminaard's face is concealed behind the grotesque mask of a Dragon Highlord—a vicious, almost machinelike visor that has a pair of wicked horns curving from the forehead. He wears shiny blue plate mail and a billowing blue cape. Standing well over 6 feet tall, Verminaard presents an imposing image of evil.

Verminaard is dedicated to the ruthless destruction of good in all its forms. No shred of conscience disturbs him in his quest for power.

He now controls all of the lands on the Abanasinian peninsula from the Seeker kingdoms to the Plains of Dergoth, and works continually to extend his power.

Ember (Pyros), an ancient, huge Red Dragon

Chaotic Evil	Hit Points 88
Armor Class -1	Movement 9″/24″
# Attacks 3	Damage 1-8/1-8/3-30
HD 11	THAC0 10
Fire Breath	Spell Use

Spells:

Level 1: *sleep, detect magic*
Level 2: *web, mirror image*
Level 3: *haste, slow*
Level 4: *polymorph other, wall of fire*

Evenstar (T'holoth), an ancient, huge Gold Dragon

Lawful Good	Hit Points 96
Armor Class -2	Movement 12″/30″
# Attacks 3	Damage 1-8/1-8/6-36
HD 12	THAC0 9
Breath Weapons (Fire, Gas)	Spell Use

Spell Book:

Level 1: *dancing lights (x2), enlarge, message, push*
Level 2: *pyrotechnics, stinking cloud*
Level 3: *phantasmal force*
Level 4: *fire charm, mnemonic enhancer*
Level 5: *rock to mud, wall of force*
Level 6: *control weather, guards and wards*

T'holoth was exiled by his people for speaking out against an oath sworn by all good dragons after the Cataclysm. His punishment was to serve as the guardian of the *Hammer of Kharas* until an ancient prophecy was fulfilled:

"When the power of the gods returns, then shall the Hammer go forth to forge once again the freedom of Krynn."

He was forced to swear to the oath he despised, then banished to the Kalil S'rith (Valley of the Thanes) to guard the Tomb of Derkin, where Kharas and the Hammer were buried after the Dwarfgate Wars.

T'holoth took the name of Evenstar in his exile, since his light was dimmed by banishment from his fellows.

Evenstar arrived to find the Tomb defenseless. Using the knowledge of his kind, he wrested the tombmound from the earth and set it in the sky. He then crafted defenses—some magical and some not—and filled the Tomb with peril.

In his loneliness, Evenstar used his magic to create life, beauty, and laughter to share the Tomb with him. In his longing, he adorned the castle with those things which brought him joy.

Evenstar has the special ability to *polymorph* at will, and changes shape frequently for pleasure. He often changes into the form of Kharas, and always does so whenever anyone enters the Tomb searching for the Hammer. Other forms he chooses include a beautiful elven maiden named Serinda, a galeb duhr, an eagle, a pony sized dog, an aghar and an opinicus. If attacked by tomb robbers, he assumes the form of a wemic, but retains his gold dragon characteristics.

Evenstar, however, is not a fighter, but a poet and dreamer. He discharges his duty faithfully, testing all who seek the Hammer until he finds those with bravery and knowledge of the true gods. Then shall he be released, and return to his own people.

Fizban the Fabulous

Eccentric Magic-User of Unknown Level

Fizban is a magic-user of indeterminate level. He appears to be senile, but was obviously once a wizard of great power. He seems to lead a charmed life. Although he always appears befuddled and absent-minded, the things Fizban does always turn out for the best—but never in the way expected.

Play Fizban for comic relief—even to his apparent death, which happens in this adventure. His true nature and purpose will be revealed in future DRAGONLANCE™ adventures.

Berem Everman, the Hunter

Fifth Level Neutral Good Ranger

Strength 12	Dexterity 12
Intelligence 15	Constitution 13
Wisdom 11	Charisma 13
THAC0 16	Hit Points 37
Armor Class 10	Movement 12″

Immune to all fire, acid, poison, magic, disease, and petrifaction. Automatically regenerates any form of damage at a rate of 1 hit point per round.

Berem has a long white beard and long dirty hair. However, beneath the concealing whiskers is the face of a middle-aged man.

Imbedded in Berem's chest, hidden by his beard, is a dull gray stone the size of a fist. It is this mysterious stone that gives him his great recuperative powers and makes him immortal.

Berem is nearly 400 years old, but he has been imprisoned away from the world for so long that he has forgotten how to speak. Only slowly does his speech return.

Berem serves a larger purpose in the great scheme of things. For now, he should remain a mystery.

arman kharas

Seventh Level Lawful Neutral Dwarf Fighter

Strength 16	Dexterity 10
Intelligence 11	Constitution 17
Wisdom 6	Charisma 9
THACO 14	Hit Points 69
Armor Class 2	Movement 6"

Wears *chain mail +2*. Carries small shield and footman's mace. Also carries a miner's pack with 100 feet of rope, hammer and chisels, sand, 12 spikes, a diamond (10 stl), a water skin, and iron rations.

A coarse black beard falls to the middle of Arman's muscular chest. A braid marking noble blood hangs to the right of his troubled face from beneath a leather skullcap. His features are worn, but the fire in his dark eyes shines bright. His left hand is calloused and bruised and his thumb is scarred. Over his armor he wears a leather jerkin tied at his knees.

Arman Kharas is son to Hornfel, patriarch of the Kytil clan, thane and prelate to the Hylar council. Fiercely loyal to his people, Arman is a dwarf with a vision and looks forward to the day when his people can return to the light.

Even though his name means "second" or "lesser" Kharas, he believes he is the literal reincarnation of Kharas, greatest hero of the Hylar. He searches for a way he can prove his legacy and become the first King of Thorbardin in hundreds of years.

---

thanes of the dwarfrealms

Once, a mighty king reigned over the nine dwarfrealms—now, the Council of Thanes rules Thorbardin. Six thanes sit on the Council: Hornfel of the Hylar, Realgar of the Theiwar, Rance of the Daergar, Gneiss of the Daewar, Tufa of the Klar, and Bluph of the Aghar. Three thrones have been taken from the Council Hall: the throne of the Neidar (7th Kingdom), vacant since the Dwarfgate Wars; the throne of the Kingdom of the Dead (8th Kingdom), which is considered to be a kingdom though without representation; and the Throne of the High King, vacant since the time of Derkin.

All the dwarfrealms agree that a strong king is needed, but none can agree on who it should be. The Hylar and their allies seek a peaceful solution, but the Theiwar and their allies seek victory by whatever means they can.

The political division of the dwarfrealms is so: the Hylar are the oldest, the leaders. The Daewar and Aghar support them, and the Klar tend to follow their lead. Against the Hylar are the Theiwar and Daergar, both of the derro race. Recently, the Theiwar were contacted by agents of Verminaard, and an unholy alliance has sprung up between the derro races and the dragon highmasters. Each side plans to double-cross the other at the first opportunity—but Realgar is unaware that Verminaard can control him.

Hornfel, thane and prelate of the Hylar, is father to Arman Kharas, and is loved by his people. He is a cautious leader and a veteran of wars. He is convinced that the days of dwarven isolation must end, and that Thorbardin must open its doors to the outside.

Realgar, a derro savant, believes himself destined to become King of Thorbardin, and pursues his goal with all available means. His alliance with Verminaard is only the latest vehicle for his ambition. He wants the dwarves to become a power to be feared.

Realgar has nine spells: *affect normal fires, blink, charm person, ESP, invisibility, paralyzation, repulsion, shadow magic,* and *wall of fog.* He also has a *cloak of protection* and a *rod of beguiling.*

Rance, War Chieftain and Thane of the Daergar, is an angry and vicious fighter who plays dirty at every opportunity. He is a dangerous man, but his temper and lack of control keep him from being the leader he dreams of being. He has a fearsome war club, encrusted with teeth, that causes double damage. His strength is 18 (75).

Gneiss, leader of the Daewar, is a war chieftain who administers his realm with a professional hand. He is calm and steady, but not an inspiring leader. His people admire and respect him, but do not love him.

Tufa, Thane of the Klar, is a modest, though respected man. He rules the Klar, a tribe of hill dwarves inside Thorbardin. Since the war with the Neidar, the Klar are at the bottom of the dwarven caste system, considered fit only for the most menial of work. He works to improve the lot of the Klar. He is allied with Hornfel, but does not wish the Klar to be puppets of anyone.

Bluph, Thane and Highbluph of the Aghar of Thorbardin, has great dignity and feels himself destined to be the first Aghar King of Thorbardin. Although actually no less stupid than the average Aghar, Bluph is considered to be a genius by his people. He is much-beloved and a great hero to the Aghar.

the hammer of kharas

The *Hammer of Kharas* is a mighty artifact. It is the only hammer that can forge a Dragonlance, and is important to the ultimate success of the heroes. It is important that this artifact not remain in the hands of the heroes! It must end up in the hands of Hornfel, Thane of the Hylar and father of Arman Kharas.

The hammer appears to be a *war hammer +2* twice normal size. It does 2d4+2 damage on a normal hit. It cannot be lifted by a person with a Strength of less than 12, and anyone with a Strength of less than 18/50 is -2 to hit with it.

The hammer acts as a *mace of disruption* against undead and creatures from the netherworld. It turns undead as a 12th level cleric.

This artifact is intelligent (I 11, Ego 11), and can control anyone who touches it if their Intelligence and Wisdom scores total less than 22.

It has the following special abilities at 20th level magic use:

Detects evil as a paladin.

Gives wielder immunity to fear, both normal and magical.

It cannot be affected by 1st to 4th level magic.

It can cast *prayer* once per day.

It provides *protection from normal missiles* once per day.

It can act as a *potion of fire giant strength* once per day.

It can *cure serious wounds* once per day.

It can inspire *magical awe* (DDG, pg. 7) in all dwarves and derro.

The hammer chooses when to activate any of its abilities.

BAAZ

FREQUENCY: *Uncommon*
 # APPEARING: *2-20*
ARMOR CLASS: *4*
MOVE: *6″/[15″]/18″*
HIT DIE: *2*
% IN LAIR: *5%*
TREASURE TYPE: *J,K,L*
ATTACKS: *1 or 2*
DAMAGE/ATTACK: *1-4/1-4*
SPECIAL ATTACKS: *None*
SPECIAL DEFENSES: *None*
MAGIC RESISTANCE: *20%*
INTELLIGENCE: *Average*
ALIGNMENT: *Lawful Evil*
SIZE: *M (5 1/2 ft.)*
PSIONIC ABILITY: *Nil*
    Modes: *Nil/Nil*
XP: *81 + 1/hp*

BOZAK

FREQUENCY: *Uncommon*
 # APPEARING: *2-20*
ARMOR CLASS: *2*
MOVE: *6″/[15″]/18″*
HIT DIE: *4*
% IN LAIR: *15%*
TREASURE TYPE: *U*
ATTACKS: *1 or 2*
DAMAGE/ATTACK: *1-4/1-4*
SPECIAL ATTACKS: *Spell use*
SPECIAL DEFENSES: *+2 saving throws*
MAGIC RESISTANCE: *20%*
INTELLIGENCE: *High*
ALIGNMENT: *Lawful Evil (some Chaotic)*
SIZE: *M (6 ft. +)*
PSIONIC ABILITY: *Nil*
    Modes: *Nil/Nil*
XP: *175 + 4/hp*

Draconians (Dragonmen)

Draconians, or dragonmen, are the basic troops of the dragon highmasters. Their origins are unknown to anyone in this section of Krynn. Three types of draconians have been encountered so far.

All draconians have wings, but the types encountered so far can truly fly for no more than one melee round. All draconians have three movement rates: walking, running on all fours while flapping their wings, and gliding. They must use all four limbs and have their wings free to use the second movement

rate. Draconians prefer to charge this way, carrying their weapons in their teeth. They can glide from any height for a distance of 4 times greater than the height from which they launch. Draconians move at a rate of 8″ in snow or ice.

Baaz: These draconians are generally the smallest of the species, and thus the easiest to pass off as humans. At the bottom of the draconian social order, they serve all other ranks of dragonmen. However, because of a quirk in their origins, these draconians often tend to be chaotic in nature and self-serving when they can get away with it.

Baaz are often encountered in disguise. They can conceal their wings under robes and, wearing a large hood and mask, can pass through civilized lands as spies. Dragon highmasters often use the Baaz in this manner just before an invasion.

When a Baaz reaches 0 hit points, he turns at once into what appears to be a stone statue. If anyone hits the stone form of the Baaz with a melee weapon, he must make a Dexterity Check at -3 or his weapon is stuck in the draconian. The statue crumbles to dust after 1-4 melee rounds have passed. Any weapons stuck in the draconian are then freed. Only the body of the Baaz turns to

DRACONIANS (DRAGONMEN)

KAPAK

FREQUENCY: *Uncommon*
APPEARING: *2-20*
ARMOR CLASS: *4*
MOVE: *6"/[15"]/18"*
HIT DIE: *3*
% IN LAIR: *5%*
TREASURE TYPE: *K,L,M*
ATTACKS: *1*
DAMAGE/ATTACK: *1-4 + poison*
SPECIAL ATTACKS: *Acid pool*
SPECIAL DEFENSES: *None*
MAGIC RESISTANCE: *20%*
INTELLIGENCE: *Average*
ALIGNMENT: *Lawful Evil*

stone and then crumbles. Any armor or weapons it carries are unaffected.

Bozak: Bozak draconians are magic-users, and have a higher resistance to magic than other draconians (see their saving throw modifier). Bozak can cast magic spells as fourth level magic-users. They are quite intelligent and very devoted to the purposes of the dragon highmasters. They never show mercy once they attack. However, they will not destroy an opponent if they believe their cause can be advanced by sparing the life.

When a Bozak reaches 0 hit points, his scaly flesh suddenly dries and crumbles from

his bones. The bones then explode, doing 1d6 points of damage to anyone within 10 ft. (no saving throw).

Kapak: Kapak draconians are distinguished by their venomous saliva, which paralyzes any creature failing a save vs. poison for 2-12 turns. They often lick the blades of their weapons (commonly shortswords) before combat, envenoming them for 3 rounds. A Kapak takes 1 full round to poison the blade again after the first venom has worn off.

Kapaks are larger than Baaz, and frequently bully and abuse their smaller cousins. The dragon highmasters endeavor to keep dif-

ferent types of draconians separated in order to prevent trouble.

When a Kapak reaches 0 hit points, his body immediately turns to acid and spreads into a 10 ft. diameter pool on the ground. Any character in the area where the Kapak died takes 1d8 points of damage per round from the acid. The acid dissolves other materials at the rate of 1 in. per round. Use the Saving Throw Matrix for Magical and Non-Magical Items in the DMG. All items possessed by the Kapak become useless.

29

Fireshadow

Frequency: *Extremely Rare*
No. Appearing: *1*
Armor Class: *0*
Move: *6"*
Hit Dice: *13+3*
% in Lair: *80%*
Treasure Type: *Nil*
No. of Attacks: *3 or 1*
Damage/Attack: *1-6/1-6/3-18 or 2-40*
Special Attacks: *See below.*
Special Defenses: *Hit only by magical weapons.*
Magic Resistance: *50%*
Intelligence: *Genius/Variable*
Alignment: *Chaotic Evil*
Size: *L (30')*
Psionic Ability: *Nil*
Attack/Defense Modes: *Nil/Nil*
Level/X. P. Value: *IX/8250+18/hp*

The fireshadow is a creature from the lower planes, and can be summoned by a chaotic evil cleric of 8th level or higher with the aid and approval of his deity.

It is made of dark, cold, green flame, and assumes whatever shape its summoner specifies.

The dark fire works like green slime: it converts flesh to dark flame on contact at a rate of 1-8 hp/round. The spread of dark flame on flesh can be stopped by a *cure* spell (cures normally), by holy water (cures 2-7 points per vial).

If a being is completely converted to dark flame, the fireshadow can control it as a smaller fireshadow (same statistics as the creature had before its death), or absorb it. Absorbed creatures restore 1d20 hit points to the fireshadow.

The fireshadow has a special attack called the *ray of oblivion*. Once, every other round, it can use this ray to inflict 16 points of damage to all in the area of effect, a save vs breath weapon will reduce the damage to half. If this damage slays its targets, their bodies are disintegrated. The ray is 1/2" wide and 13" long.

The fireshadow cannot be turned, but a *mace of disruption* affects it as a vampire. The *Hammer of Kharas* can destroy it.

It is immune to firebased attacks. The dark flame causes 1d6 points of damage to all creatures within 10 feet 9 (No save, but fire resistance applies).

The fireshadow's biggest nemesis is the light of day, which will utterly destroy it within 1d4 rounds.

The Dwarves of Thorbardin

There are seven major races of dwarves in the land of Krynn: the Hylar, the Theiwar, the Daewar, the Daergar, the Neidar, the Klar, and the Aghar.

The Hylar

The Hylar are mountain dwarves, the oldest and most noble of the dwarven races of Thorbardin. Most of the great dwarven kings have been Hylar, including both Derkin and Kharas. Even in the dark days since the Cataclysm, the Hylar retain great influence. Most Hylar live in the famous Life-Tree, an incredible feat of dwarven engineering. The Hylar invented many of the mechanical devices for which the dwarves are justly famous.

The Theiwar

The Theiwar are derro, a strange degenerate dwarf race. They hate light and suffer from nausea in sunlight. Nevertheless, their dreams are of world conquest and domination. Of the dwarven races, they are the most concerned with spells and magic—most of their leaders are savants with spell-casting powers.

The Theiwar consider themselves the highest of the derro kingdoms, and seek to wrest leadership of Thorbardin away from the Hylar. They look forward to winning by whatever means are closest to hand—even civil war.

The Daewar

The Daewar are mountain dwarves, like the Hylar. They are justly respected, and many important leaders have come from their midst. The Daewar are great soldiers, and were at the forefront in the Dwarfgate Wars. In peacetime, they defer leadership to the Hylar, but take an active interest in public safety and public works.

The Daergar

The Daergar are derro who split off from the Theiwar many hundreds of years ago. Their culture has flourished, and now they are powerful in Thorbardin. They are, if possible, even more evil and dangerous than their Theiwar cousins, favoring murder, torture, and thievery to get their way. Their leader is always the most powerful warrior of the Daergar kingdom, "elected" in a bloody combat.

The Neidar

The Neidar are the hill dwarves who lived outside Thorbardin at the time of the Cataclysm. Based on old treaties, they felt they had the right to seek refuge in the kingdom, but Thorbardin could not absorb all the Neidar. Thus came the tragic Dwarfgate Wars, which pitted brother against brother. Hatred between the Neidar and the dwarves of Thorbardin continues to this day.

The Klar

The Klar are hill dwarves who lived inside Thorbardin at the time of the Dwarfgate Wars. Following the wars, the Klar were deprived of property and persecuted terribly for their supposed sympathy for the Neidar (in fact, many Klar fought with bravery in the war). Now, they serve the wealthy dwarves of Thorbardin in menial roles. After centuries of suffering, they look for leadership to deliver them.

The Aghar

The ludicrous Aghar, or gully dwarves, are the lowest class in the dwarven caste system. Other dwarves and humans find them comical for their stupidity (few can count higher than two) and their incredible egos. They work in menial, dirty tasks, but that is all they are qualified to do.

The Kingdom of the Dead

The dwarves venerate their dead, and consider the kingdom of the dead to be the 8th Kingdom. This has little practical effect on politics, but has a profound effect on dwarven thinking about the afterlife. Dwarves use a variety of divination methods—some are real, but many are just superstition.

The High King

The last dwarven kingdom is that of the High King of the Dwarves. The high throne has been vacant since the days of Derkin, and no one has yet managed to claim it, though many have tried.